FINDING MY WAY:

Positivity
Through Adversity

by

Nick Porter

DORRANCE
PUBLISHING CO
EST. 1920
PITTSBURGH, PENNSYLVANIA 15238

Dorrance Publishing Co
585 Alpha Drive
Pittsburgh, PA 15238
Visit our website at *www.dorrancebookstore.com*

ISBN: 978-1-6376-4340-2
eISBN: 978-1-6376-4652-6

Prologue

WAKE UP. GET UP. MAKE A DIFFERENCE IN YOUR LIFE. DON'T ever let negativity stand in your way. It took me almost fifty years to finally learn to live with this in mind. We do get wiser with age, and everything in my life is better because of my experiences. We can't go back and change things, but if we learn from our past, we can forge a better path for our future.

As I was writing this book, it got me thinking about the number of people I've met along the way. There is no way to come up with a finite number, but each person had some impact on my life. Obviously, some more than others. Every blood relative, friend, teacher, coach, co-worker, boss, acquaintance, fraternity brother, teammate, stranger, girlfriend, in-law, and my one and only wife, Colleen.

My hope for you in reading my story is to take what the late basketball coach, Jim Valvano, said on national television March 4, 1993, just weeks before his death. "To me, there are three things we all should do every day. We should do every day of our lives. Number one is *laugh*. You should laugh every day. Number two is *think*. You should spend some time in thought. Number three is, you should have your *emotions moved to tears*, could be happiness or joy. But think about it. If you laugh, you think, and you cry, that's a full day. That's a heck of a day. You do that seven days a week, you're going to have something special."

To this day, I remember that speech vividly. I remember watching it live on ESPN. I can almost recite it word for word. It wasn't until a few years ago that I started to really think about it. I try to do these three things every single day of my life. I hope my story can make those three things happen for you.

Been There Done That

BEFORE YOU CAN MOVE FORWARD, SOMETIMES IT'S BEST TO look back on your life and understand how you got to this point, and how you can move forward.

I was raised a Catholic in an upper-middle class family in the suburbs of St. Louis. I attended Catholic grade school (St. Clement) and a Jesuit High School (St. Louis University High Class of 1986). I never wanted for anything. Like most good Catholic families, most families in my neighborhood had multiple children. We were no different, as I had four sisters and a brother. I was fourth of the six. My dad made sure to make all of us work and earn money, because he was not going to "hand out" money to us. I played a lot of sports like baseball, basketball, soccer and golf. It was golf that I gravitated to as I got older.

I remember when I was around eight years old sneaking on the local, public golf course, Crystal Lake. My brother and I would carry our golf clubs through Berkley Manor (our neighborhood) and make our way to the third hole. We would wait for an opening and cross over to the course through the bushes. We did this many times, but sometimes we would also pay to play. When I was twelve, I heard about a private golf course called Westwood Country Club. They had the best caddie program in the area, so my brother and I signed up and went through the classes in order to caddie there during the summers. This was so awesome because it was the same year, 1980, that the movie *Caddyshack* was released. The golf club in the movie was named

Bushwood. It was so much like Westwood. I kid you not, the caddie house was a chaotic mess of misfits. There were over the road truck drivers, pot smokers, high school dropouts, and punk ass kids, like me, fighting over "loops." Loops are caddie slang for a round of eighteen holes. Each round of golf netted me $8. As I got older and stronger, I would double loop and make $16. If I was lucky, I would literally get my $0.50 tip just like Danny Noonan got from Judge Smailes in *Caddyshack*. The best part of the job was playing free golf on Mondays. Private golf clubs are closed on Mondays, so I would have my mom drop me off early in the morning and come back at dusk to pick me up. I was starting to become a pretty good player, and every year there was a caddie golf day where we had an eighteen-hole tournament, BBQ, and use of the pool. Unlike the movie, they allowed us more than fifteen minutes to swim, just as long as we left the *Baby Ruth* bars out of the pool. I was fortunate enough to pull a "Noonan" and win the caddie tournament. Just like the movie, that came with perks like caddying for the best players on Saturdays and Sundays. I was being requested as a caddie, and by age fourteen, I was showing up for tee times instead of having to wait it out for a loop. It was at this time that I also started caddying in local amateur tournaments at other courses in the area. My parents also played golf, and since they saw how my brother and I loved the game so much, they joined a country club named *Forest Hills*. This club was known for their junior golf program, and it became my summer hangout on Fridays (junior golf day). My dad also enjoyed the gin rummy games on Tuesday nights.

When I turned sixteen and was able to drive, golf became my life. I quit caddying at Westwood and found a job working the bag room at *Greenbriar Hills Country Club*. I continued to caddie in local tournaments and played as much golf as I could at both *Forest Hills* and *Greenbriar Hills*. I played high school golf for three years, but as far as school went, I never took it serious. *St. Louis University High* was one of the premier, private Jesuit schools in the country. Classwork was not easy, especially when you don't apply yourself. Needless to say, by the end of my sophomore year and into my junior year, my grades were nearing the "Hoover" level. Hoover was a character from the movie *Animal House*. There's a great scene where Dean Wormer berates the Delta fraternity for their grades. When he gets to Hoover, he says, "Mr. Hoover, President of the Delta House, four C's and a F. 1.6 GPA. A fine example you set." That was where I was, and the administrators were threatening to kick me out, unless I enrolled in an outside class at the *Institute for Motivational Development*. My dad approached me about it, and obviously, I was against it. However, he cared little about my opinion. This was the only way I was going to be allowed to stay enrolled at "The U-High." So I went to the class, and the first thing they made me do was take an I.Q. test. I knew I wasn't a dumb guy, and when I scored a 139, it pretty much solidified what I thought and probably shocked some people at *St. Louis U. High*. Although it shouldn't have, because I scored in the top 10 percent on my entrance exam to get in the school, and that shocked my eighth grade teacher.

The humiliating part of this class was next. Some of you may remember the talk show, *Sally Jesse Raphael?* The lady with the obnoxious, red glasses and blond hair. In my opinion, she was just a female version of Jerry Springer. Anyway, she got her start in St. Louis. She did a show titled *Underachieving Teenagers*, and she asked the President of *the Institute for Motivational Development* to be a guest and bring a graduate of the program with him. Who do you think they called? That's correct, lucky me. You can bet your ass I tried to talk my way out of that, but to no avail. So my parents, sister and I all went downtown to the NBC affiliate to tape this ridiculously, insane and extremely worthless show. We weren't the only ones there for a taping, so they put us in the "green room" to watch the episode being taped before ours. It was Heloise from *Hints from Heloise* fame. I don't even remember why she was on the show? I think to give some lifestyle tip about health? Who the hell knows? In the "green room" they have a TV to watch the show, and my dad is sitting next to me, and another guy, who I just assumed was Heloise's husband or manager? I never asked. I could tell as my dad watched and listened to her that he so desperately wanted to blurt out, "Who the hell is this lady?" Thankfully, I whispered just in time, "Don't say a word."

It was now my turn to get on stage. My parents and sister went out and sat in the audience. I was bound and determined to make this the biggest joke I could. I didn't want to be there. I was seventeen and it was my senior year. The last thing I wanted any of my friends to see was this embarrassment. Sally started off with questions for my parents and me, to which I gave basically one word answers. I was like that athlete getting interviewed that looked like a deer in headlights. At the first commercial break, they removed me from the stage and Sally conversed with the President of I.M.D. What teenage kid wants to go on national television and talk about being an underachiever? The best part of all this was the show was aired in St. Louis during my Spring Break. I was in Florida with almost all the other kids from St. Louis schools. I'm not really sure if anyone I know saw it? Maybe a handful of people. I did get a tape of the show, which I destroyed, and since Sally hasn't been on the air for a long time, there likely are no other tapes to be found. I wasn't an underachiever. I just didn't care for school too much. My English teacher failed a few of us, so in order to get our high school diploma, we had to take a college English class at the community college. This took place in the summer after graduation ceremonies. I got all dressed up in a tuxedo, went to my graduation, walked across stage to get my diploma, and when I got back to my seat I opened it up. It was empty! Long story short. I got an "A" in the English class, and my high school English teacher didn't return the following school year. Logically, my next step would be to find something to do other than go to college. WRONG!

The University of Mississippi was college stop #1. I knew almost immediately this path was going sideways. My parents drove me to Oxford, moved me in my dorm room, and they returned to St. Louis. About eight hours later, after bar hopping with some new "friends" I met, I was found passed out on the hood of a campus police car. Luckily for me, the police officer sent me on my way back to the dorm. Four months and forty pounds later, I came home for Christmas and transferred to college stop #2, The University of Missouri at Columbia. Twelve months in a real life Animal House fraternity had me for a quick exit. Let me recall what I accomplished at Mizzou. After further review, in order not to embarrass myself any further, nothing. I officially realized that school was not meant for me at this time of my life. In order to make some quick money and allow me to think about my life, my dad got me a job as a "roughneck" on his oil rig in Northern Kansas. Winter time in Kansas working the graveyard shift (8p-8a) on a freaking oil rig. Temps were so cold that I had to use a blow torch most of my shift to heat the pipes so water could pump in the hole. I spent three months in some flea bag motel in Tonganoxie, Kansas. When I wasn't working, I was either shooting pool at a local bar or sleeping. Some weekends I would make the drive to Lawrence and hang out with some high school buddies who were in school at *Kansas University*. I finally had an awakening while standing on an ice covered deck, when I dropped a forty-eight-inch wrench into a three-foot wide hole that was 1500 feet deep, that this was not my calling. I had slipped on the ice while straddling the hole. It was either me or that wrench going down. I chose the latter. One of the best decisions I made in my life to that point.

When spring rolled around, I made a call to my old boss at *Greenbriar Hills* to see if I could come back and work there. He offered me a job as the Assistant Golf Professional. I was excited because I really wanted to get involved with golf in some capacity.

I spent three years at *Greenbriar Hills*. I learned the business side of running a pro shop, learned the game in ways I didn't know, passed my playing ability test, played in local professional events, and began to give lessons to earn extra money. I had moved into my own condo, was paying my own bills, and learning life lessons on the fly. I may not have been learning the best way, but it really was something I don't regret. Not many guys my age could handle this, but I was maturing much quicker than I would have if I stayed in school. Those three years at *Greenbriar Hills* were times I will never forget. My boss, Scott Oulds, treated me like his son, and the members all treated me like I was one of their own.

Another thing I will never forget is the weekend I spent working with the United States Secret Service. You read that correctly. In today's world, no civilian would be able to walk off the street and get up close and personal with the President of the United States, but in 1992, that's what I was allowed to do. A friend of mine, Jim Quist, was working for Missouri Senator Christopher "Kit" Bond, and they needed some volunteers to assist with President George H. W. Bush, aka *TIMBERWOLF*, for the Presidential Debates at Washington University in St. Louis. The Secret Service uses code names for Presidents and their family.

Jim recruited me and John Strubert, another friend of mine from St. Clement. It was the most surreal weekend of my life. After passing a background check, we were assigned to meet at the Drury Hotel in downtown St. Louis. My job was to drive Press Secretary, Marlin Fitzwater, in the vehicle behind the President's limousine. The motorcade started at the hotel and proceeded to Lambert International Airport. The entire drive we had the highway to ourselves. Every single off and on ramp was blocked by police so we could drive unimpeded. I drove that big, black Suburban onto the tarmac within ten yards of Air Force One. Government agents and/or military were lined up on roof tops of some of the hangars. That's one big ass plane, especially that close to it. I remember it being a nice October Sunday, and as we got closer to *Washington University*, the streets were lined with people. Rolling down Skinker Blvd. past Forest Park and making the left hand turn on Forest Park Parkway, there were people holding signs and lined two or three deep on the sidewalk. As we turned on to Big Bend Blvd., we parked right outside the auditorium side door. President Bush was debating Bill Clinton and Ross Perot that evening. All of the drivers had to stay with their vehicles outside the Field House doors, just in case of an emergency. We watched the debate from closed circuit television. I never got to talk into my cuff or collar like the real Secret Service agents, but it was still a very fun weekend. I sported the dark suit and sunglasses well.

The next few years, I began another chapter of my life. I enrolled at a local broadcast school in St. Louis. The school had their own radio station, 770 WEW. This was a Big Band station that played the likes of Glenn Miller, Duke Ellington, and Tommy Dorsey. While in school, I was asked to read the newscasts and eventually had my own show, which I called, "Nick at Night." That didn't go over well with the Nickelodeon folks, so I had to drop that show title. I didn't even know anyone was listening, much less the local cable outlet. Part of my job required me to attend live, local big band concerts. Imagine the shock when the listeners, mostly retired people, showed up and saw a punk twenty-four-year-old introducing the bands? They had no idea I was that young. I always had another on-air talent from the station with me, so I never had to do that on my own.

Anyway, I flew through the program in less than a year, and in 1993 I landed a job at the sports radio station, 590AM KFNS. Sports radio was in the infant stages, and it was fun to be involved with it. It was a low paying job, but I quickly learned a lot about the business. I was told I had a voice for radio, and we shared a studio with one of the larger, FM Adult Contemporary music stations, KEZK. One of the engineer/producers who handled the commercial voice work for both stations gave me a shot at voicing local commercials. It would be nice to still have some of these on tape, but I never saved any of them. So after a year, they gave me some producing roles, on air work, postgame show hosting duties for the St. Louis Cardinals and Blues, and in 1994, the now defunct U.S. OLYMPIC FESTIVAL was in St. Louis. Events like kayak and canoe racing were held at *Six Flags Thunder River*. Softball games at the fields in North County, Boxing at *The Fabulous Fox Theater* and figure skating at the *Arena*, with baseball at *Busch Stadium*. I can't remember all the events, but nevertheless, it was a huge success in our town.

Also, that summer, I caddied for a family friend, Don Walsworth, in the 1994 United States Open Golf Tournament at Oakmont Country Club outside Pittsburgh. I caddied for Don at the sectional qualifier in St. Louis at Old Warson Country Club. He was the low qualifier, or medalist as they call it, and we were on our way to his and my first U.S. OPEN experience. I remember that vividly, as Pittsburgh was in the midst of a major heat wave. Temperatures were in the mid-nineties with high humidity. Walking those hills of Pennsylvania on a golf course of 7000 yards became a survival of the fittest. It was so bad that by the end of the day my pants were soaking wet. Players, caddies and spectators all were trying to avoid heat stroke. The side stories at this event were numerous. This was Arnold Palmer's last U.S. Open. He grew up down the road in Latrobe. He played his first U.S. OPEN there as an amateur in 1953 at the age of twenty-three. This was also the week of the famous O.J. Simpson scene in the White Bronco. I remember sitting in the hotel and watching that play out on TV. The World Cup was also being played across the U.S., as were the NBA finals and the NHL parade in New York City celebrating the Rangers title.

One of the funnier moments I had was walking to the parking lot with my player's golf clubs. You don't see caddies wearing long pants anymore because the PGA changed the rules allowing caddies to wear shorts after this heat wave ordeal. Players get free rental cars and park in their own lot. Kids would always run up to them asking for autographs. I was by myself as Don was still in the locker room. So two boys, thinking I'm a player, approach me for my autograph. I tried to tell them I was just the caddie, but they weren't buying it. So I signed my name and off they went. If you saw my signature you would know that those two boys to this day are trying to figure out who the hell I am? It's a scribbly mess. But the week went on and Don did quite well. He shot 71 on Thursday and 75 on Friday. We had a little scare on Friday on our eighteenth hole. Don drove his ball in the fairway and then the siren went off signaling a stoppage in play. It was late in the day, and the heat produced a pop-up thunderstorm. We marked the ball with three tees in the ground and walked off the course. We had to come back Saturday morning at 7:00 to finish the hole and the round. Since we were one of the last groups on the course, we knew the cut line. Don could make no worse than a bogey five to make the cut. When we arrived Saturday morning to finish, the grounds crew made the mistake of cutting the fairways for Round Three. They ran over Don's tees where he marked the ball. The head rules official told Don he now had to drop his ball as close to where we thought it was. This was bullshit, and I let the official know it. Why were they cutting grass and changing the course before Round Two was officially over? So when Don did drop his ball, it rolled into a divot, which is a mark made from a previous shot that takes the grass out of the ground. Basically he had to hit his shot off dirt. Don dug deep and ended up making a bogey five. He made the cut and we stuck around for the weekend.

Saturday's pairing was with Steven Richardson out of England and Sunday we were paired with Tom Lehman. I had met Tom a couple years before, and Don knew him quite well from his college and now professional playing days. I can't explain the rush it is to be inside the ropes caddying in a U.S. OPEN on such an historic course. Don finished the weekend 73-77 and tied for forty-fourth. What made it even better was Don allowing me to stay with him at the player's hotel, so I had the chance to meet a few players, like Ben Crenshaw, Constantino Rocca, Ian Woosnam and Ernie Els. Els was a newcomer to the Tour, roughly twenty-three years old. He would end up winning the tournament in a Monday final that lasted twenty holes. It was a three-man playoff between Loren Roberts and Colin Montgomerie. After ninety-two holes, five days and scorching temps, the week came to a close, and we did it all again in 1995. I met Don in Kansas City to caddie in the Sectional Qualifier at *Milburn Country Club*. He finished second and grabbed one of the spots for the 1995 U.S. OPEN at *Shinnecock Hills* up near the Hamptons of Long Island, New York. That was a great experience as well. Don didn't fare as well, and we didn't make the weekend cut, but I did get to walk eighteen holes with Tom Watson in a practice round. That was a treat to watch him play, but it was also beneficial to me as a caddie because Mr. Watson had the best caddie in the business, Bruce Edwards. In those eighteen holes he was gracious and informative. He taught me how to best mark a course for yardage, the areas to hit to, and just a general view of what a good caddie needs to do. Bruce would later be diagnosed with Lou Gehrig's Disease (Amyotrophic Lateral Sclerosis or ALS) in 2003. He succumbed to it on April 8, 2004 at age forty-nine. Far too young and talented. Meanwhile, Don and Mr. Watson have a lot in common. Both are from Missouri. Both were Missouri State Amateur Champions. Mr. Watson a four-time winner in 1967, 1968, 1970 and 1971. That last victory was actually at *Milburn Country Club*. Don won the event in 1985. Both men also played golf at Stanford University where Don won the 1986 PAC-10 Individual title. Mr. Watson, well, he went on to have a hall of fame golf career. Now both men reside in the Overland Park, Kansas area and Don runs the family business and gave up his pro status to play as an amateur again.

After the summer of 1995, I found myself at a crossroads. I began dating a girl at the beginning of the year, my job was paying me next to nothing for the hours I was putting in, and I was approaching twenty-eight years old. I had no college degree, so finding a "real" job was going to be hard. I took the leap and quit my radio job and was hired as a salesman at a local business selling advertising. I did that for a while and didn't like it. It was later in 1998 or 1999 when my father decided to sell his financial consulting business and buy a chain of dry cleaners. He offered me a job to help run them and I accepted. More on this story later.

1999 was a big year for me. I enrolled in college in May, worked days at the dry cleaners, went to school at night, and got married in November. In September 2000, my wife and I welcomed our first child, Andrew, and in January 2001 we bought our first house, and I graduated college in May. I then quit the dry cleaners and began a now twenty-year career in sales. We moved into a bigger house in 2006 and had three more wonderful children, Eve, Grant and Tessa. Life was good. That doesn't mean we didn't have our bumps along the way like every married couple and family. There were miscarriages, numerous lost jobs or changing jobs, financial struggles, child illnesses and arguments. But somehow, we always made it through to live another day.

So why did I take you through this journey of my early life? For one, I'm not sure how many people in this world have lived a life like this? And this was the abbreviated and PG version. Secondly, I believe it's essential to learn from your past in order to move forward in life. In order to find your way, you need to have a direction. That direction is dictated by your past experiences. Once you know what you want in life, you can then begin your journey. I look back on my experiences now much differently than I did when I was living them. I was a mess. I was a borderline alcoholic who quit many things thinking something better was on the other side. That doesn't mean my early life was bad or wasteful. I look at it as the path that led me to where I am today. One slight change in my first twenty-seven years likely doesn't lead me to having my wife and children with me today. If you play that "what if" game, you are wasting your time and energy. December 26, 2017 would be my fiftieth birthday, but seventeen days prior to that, life threw my family a punch in the gut.

This Was
No Hangover

IT WAS A SATURDAY MORNING, AND I WAS FRESH OFF THE FIRST Christmas party of the season. Like most parties, there was a lot of eating and drinking. However, waking up this particular Saturday was different than any other, because I could barely get myself out of bed. I told Colleen that my lower right side was in excruciating pain. I thought maybe it was something I ate the night before? After all, the Christmas party was a smorgasbord of shrimp, White Castles, Taco Bell, wings and every dip known to mankind. Mix in a truckload of local Anheuser-Busch products and various spirits, and you have a good old fashioned, St. Louis holiday tradition.

Or, maybe it was appendicitis? It was in the correct spot. No matter what I thought it was, I promised my dad that I would be at his house first thing in the morning to split wood. It was our annual tradition to make sure he had enough wood to burn from December to April, seven days a week and twenty-four hours a day. So I got dressed and walked gingerly to the car to make the thirty-minute drive.

It could have been twenty degrees that morning, I don't rightfully recall? I was in so much pain that my body made it feel like it was ninety outside. When I made it to his house, I walked in and said to him, "Dad, I'm not sure how long I will make it today, but I'll go as long as I can." My dad replied, "What the hell is wrong with you?" I said, "I'm just not feeling that well. My stomach is in a lot of discomfort." You have to know my dad to appreciate the dialog here. This is an eighty-year-old man, with a slight twang in his voice, from a small town in Northwest Missouri. He was used to his other son coming up with fifty excuses not to perform manual labor, so he didn't want to hear it from me. By the way, my older brother was not there. So he asked what I did last night. I said, "Colleen and I went to Kevin's annual Christmas party." The immediate response was, "Dammit Nicky, you're just hung over. Get your gloves and let's go." I always know the conversation is going nowhere when "Nicky" is called out, but I had to respond with, "Dad, I've had enough hangovers in my life, and this is no hangover."

So outside we went and got that log splitter cranked up. What the hell did people do before the invention of that machine? Oh, I remember. Kids watched their father split wood with a maul and wedge as they lifted, carried and stacked the wood. At least this is how we did it from 1975 to 1995. So we proceeded to continue splitting wood, but as the morning moved along, my dad did notice I was moving a little slow. We took breaks every thirty minutes and would turn off the splitter and go inside. We did this about four times, and since I get my stubbornness from my dad, I kept going back for more. But then, almost like God was trying to tell me to pull my head out of my ass and go seek medical attention, the pull cord on the splitter ripped off when we tried to start it. In the glorious words of Chevy Chase as Clark Griswold from the movie *Christmas Vacation*, the words in my mind screamed out, "Hallelujah! Holy Shit! Where's the Tylenol?"

But the fun was just beginning, because at that time, I must have been delusional. I had promised Kevin the night before at his party that I would bring him some firewood. So I loaded up the truck and headed to his house. I might have broken the speed limit a half dozen times on that drive, but I was bound to make the delivery. I told Kevin I was feeling ill, and I would unload the wood, stack it, and go home. When I got home, I thought a nice, hot shower would make me feel better. Why not? Hot showers are a cure all for everything in my book. After the shower, I laid down with hopes of going off into a deep sleep and waking up realizing this was all just a nightmare.

Wrong again. It was nearing 3:00 in the afternoon and nothing was getting better. I mentioned to Colleen that maybe it was time to take me to the E.R.? She agreed, because right then, I could barely walk. Both of us were thinking the log splitting escapade may have burst my appendix. Colleen pulled up to the automatic doors of the E.R., and it took me over a minute just to get out of the car. Almost on all fours walking like a dog, I was able to get in the hospital as twenty to thirty people stared at me like I was some kind of wounded animal. Technically, I was.

The good thing about the E.R. is they will get the more serious patients in as quickly as possible. I filled out the paperwork like a student who didn't study writes answers on a test, or some eighteen year-old filling in the "C" circles on their ACT test. For all I know, I could have written my name as Ricky Bobby from Talladega, Alabama on those forms. All I wanted was to find out what this pain was and how to make it go away? So off to the exam room I went. After poking and prodding from the nurse and doctor, they sent me in for a CT scan. When the results came back, they told me they needed to admit me to the hospital now and get me on antibiotics. The colon was so swollen they couldn't even see the appendix. Just hearing the word, "antibiotic" put me in some comfort. Relief was not far away, so now it was just time to grin and bear it. I still had no idea what was heading my way. I was still planning on an appendectomy.

Once I was admitted to my room and hooked up to the drugs, the discomfort started to subside. Since it was a Saturday, the hospital was fairly quiet. I was told the antibiotics would need seventy-two hours to get the swelling down. A surgeon and a gastrointestinal doctor would be in on Monday to review the scan and talk to me about my condition. I knew one thing for certain. This was no hangover.

Making It Better

MAKE THINGS BETTER. THOSE THREE WORDS ARE WHAT INSPIRE me today. I always cringe when I hear the phrase, "It is what it is". That is a cop out for people who are too lazy to make an effort to change and make things better than what they are. Take it upon yourself not to accept the status quo and find a way to, "make what IT is, Better". Imagine if our forefathers, like Ben Franklin, George Washington, and Thomas Jefferson lived by the creed, "it is what it is"? Or if Abraham Lincoln decided that slavery was acceptable? The examples are endless. Our country was founded by the idea NOT to accept what they were told to do and how they were told to do it.

It took over two years for me to start writing this book because I really wasn't sure how it was going to end. Once I realized there may not be an official ending, it was time to get busy writing. Friends and family read my updates on social media and kept telling me to write a book. The only problem I had was how to approach it and tell my story? Each chapter is based on certain moments of my life, what I learned, and why it was so important.

How did I get to this point of my life and why am I writing this? The answer is simple. We all have that moment in our life that makes us realize what we can be instead of who we are. Some people find it at a young age, but it took me longer to figure it out. I have always felt there was something missing in my life. I enjoy talking to people. Helping people. Being around people. I don't have endless financial means, so philanthropy hasn't been an option. However, I do have the desire to pay it forward in other ways. This book is one step in that process for me, but you will also learn as you read this that I've found it very helpful to be open with my battle. I found it helpful and healthier to just be an "open book" with what I was going through on a daily basis. Maybe that made some people uncomfortable? Maybe some others found it annoying. But what you should know if you are battling cancer or any possible life threatening illness, is this: It's about YOU first. That may sound selfish, but as you progress, you will learn this is your life. How do you want to live? The chapters in here will fill you in on what to possibly expect, and it's been a learning experience for me that I know me better than anyone. I've absolutely learned more about who I am, who I want to be, and how I want to live the remaining years I have left above ground. I'll fill you in on a little secret that many people don't realize. You are stronger than you think you are. You have a mental toughness that just needs to be tapped into on a regular basis. Before I got cancer, I thought of myself as tougher than most. I experienced a lot in the first forty-nine years of my life. However, the last three years have been a life changing experience, not because I got cancer, but because I owned the cancer and learned how strong the mind is over the body.

I hope you enjoy this story. At times, I'll try to bring some humor into it, and of course, it will have plenty of the reality that is, cancer. It's not just a story about me. It's about my support team as well. I will fill in the blanks about everyone and everything that's gone on for the last three-plus years.

C-Day to D-Day

DECEMBER 11, 2017. A MAN WITH A VERY SERIOUS LOOK ON his face walked into my hospital room at 5:00 P.M. Unlike the doctor in the "AT&T" commercial, he looked better than okay. I consider myself a good judge of character, and I also tend to spot things that seem a little concerning. I could tell he was about to deliver some news that he didn't want to say, nor did my wife and I want to hear. He introduced himself as Dr. David Nickel, and I introduced myself and Colleen. Then, I immediately said to him, "Doc, you look like you have something serious to say, so don't beat around the bush. Just spit it out." He replied, "I looked at your scan and blood work with the G.I. Doctor, and I'm 99 percent sure you have colon cancer." I looked at my wife, paused for about five seconds, and just replied, "How do you know?" I was curious as to how that came about when up until that weekend, I never experienced any symptoms of colon cancer. No problems going to the bathroom. No blood in my stool. No fatigue. So curiosity got the best of me. All of these things came to mind, especially since the nurse practitioner had previously told me I had a gallbladder issue. He replied, "There's a blockage in your colon, your white blood count is extremely low, your hemoglobin count is extremely low, and twenty-two years of being a doctor, so I'm 99 percent sure that's the problem we are dealing with." All I could think about right then and there is, "Okay Doc, how do we take care of it?' This guy was prepared and professional. He mapped out a plan right there for us to hear, and let me tell you, it went like clockwork from that point to the time I was discharged. The plan had me sent home from the hospital on Tuesday, start colonoscopy prep at home on Wednesday, come back Thursday at 11:00 for a colonoscopy, and then surgery the next day at 12:00.

Now that we knew what was wrong with me, it came time to decide how we would handle the news? We agreed to call our families and tell them. After all, we had been at the hospital for forty-eight hours, so it's not like we could hide from this. Family and friends were concerned, and it was the right thing to do for us. We didn't feel the need to keep others worrying. Colleen and I both called our parents, siblings and a few friends. I just remember it being very emotional. I really can't recall what I said exactly, but I do remember asking my friend, Mike Christian, to let others know what was going on. It was presented to me by the hospital staff to let my wife and family handle it from here. Through text, email and social media, Colleen took care of it. Thinking about that now seems so selfish. I'm sure that was not easy for her, but I did know that we would have a tremendous support group in our corner. The outpouring of love, prayers and hope was incredible.

That night was tough to sleep. Colleen went home to take care of the children, and I laid there in bed with a thousand thoughts going through my mind. Guilt, frustration, confusion and anger were just a few emotions I experienced. It was Christmas time, I thought I was a healthy forty-nine-year-old man, and then out of nowhere this knocks me and my family down a few notches. However, one thing always kept coming back to me. It helps nobody to be pissed off. I started thinking I didn't want to be that guy who kept saying, "Why me?" Those two words needed to be eliminated from my vocabulary, because there is no way in hell I wanted this to happen to Colleen or my children. So why not me? If I had to watch one of them go through this, then that would be the toughest thing in my life. Nothing made me more special than anyone else. I wouldn't wish this on my worst enemy, and this was just going to be another challenge in my life I had to overcome. It wasn't going to be easy, and I knew I wouldn't be alone in my fight. God gives us all challenges, and He wouldn't give you anything you couldn't handle. At least that's what I always believed and still do. On the flip side, those that do survive cancer may ask themselves, "Why am I alive? How come I'm here and others weren't so fortunate?" If you play this back and forth game in your mind, you will drive yourself crazy. You can't play God. You can't question how or why? All you can do is wake up every day, get out of bed, and go live your life to the fullest. This YOLO, (You Only Live Once), is a bunch of nonsense. You only die once. You live every day.

So the dreaded "C-DAY" (cancer day) needed to turn the page to "D-DAY" really quick. Tuesday, December 12, 2017, marked the day Team Porter began the fight to DESTROY cancer. Dig in, dig deep, destroy and defeat cancer. Any word that began with a "D" was in my vocabulary to defeat this disease, DAMMIT!

The First 40

IT WAS TIME TO GO HOME FOR ABOUT THIRTY-SIX HOURS, AND while it was nice to be home, I found myself spending most of my time becoming one with the toilet. After a night of sleep Tuesday at home, the next day and night would be one big learning experience. Wednesday was colonoscopy prep day. I knew when I picked up my "colon blow" at the pharmacy I was in trouble. This thing looked like a milk jug on steroids. One hundred fluid ounces of the second worst, foul tasting crap you can ever drink. Barium sulfate is the worst thing you can put in your body (as I found out later). Anyway, if you've ever had a colonoscopy, you know what I'm talking about...maybe? I say maybe because Colleen later had a colonoscopy and her "colon blow elixir" looked like a Gatorade bottle. Thirty-two ounces. So my Gastrointestinal Doctor really needed me "cleaned out" judging from what he prescribed. So without going into all the details, I'll just ask you this, "Have you ever seen the movie, *Shawshank Redemption?* If so, my "insides" made a cameo appearance when Andy Dufresne crawled through the sewer of shit smelling foulness. That is all.

Needless to say, you don't get to sleep much when you are taking this. My colonoscopy was scheduled for 11:00 Thursday morning, and the directions for the colon prep began twelve hours prior. It called for staggered ten minute intervals the first hour. Ten ounces at a time. I didn't feel anything for an hour, and I even commented to Colleen that it didn't seem to be "working." Well, little did I know that ten minutes after saying that, the levee was breached. Once that round of magic ended, it was now time to finish the other half of the bottle. By 7:00 A.M., an all-clear was sounded and it was time to get ready for "Doc Proc" to do his thing.

I figured the colonoscopy couldn't be anything near as interesting as the prep work. Besides, I was too tired to even think about it. Colleen and I spent about thirty minutes in the prep room listening to the nurses and doctor tell us how this worked. I didn't really care how it worked, but more importantly, just get in there and find out what we're dealing with. What we were dealing with was three tumors and a couple polyps. The tumors were indeed cancerous and fairly good size. The surgeon's prediction was correct. He already had the operating room reserved for the next day at 12:00. I was admitted to the hospital in what would eventually become another eight days.

Surgery day was upon us. Once again, all morning, nurses and doctors came in and out of the room laying out "the plan." I do have a newfound respect for everyone on a hospital staff because they really do have a lot of responsibility and pressure on them. So to my baby sister, Holly, kudos to you for what you do every single day. I'm very proud of you.

Now that the poking, prodding and paperwork was complete, it was time to wheel me down to pre-op. The surgeon told us that he was going to begin with a laparoscopic procedure making three incisions and try to remove any and all tumors he could. If he felt that wasn't the best option, he would need to cut me open. Once again, I appreciated all the insight and information, and I didn't care how it worked. I just knew he was the expert, and I put my trust in him. I got to say my "goodbyes" to my wife, children, parents and in-laws. I never thought this was the last goodbye, but as in any surgery, you just never know? I'm a crier and not ashamed of it. I will get to that later in the book, but that was a tough moment for me.

A few hours later, after waking up in post-op, the surgeon came in to tell me how the operation went. The laparoscopy wasn't an option. He had to cut me open and remove twelve inches of my colon and re-attach it. Medical term is a colon re-section. Thankfully, it was on the ascending side (opposite the rectum) of the colon, which made it much easier and didn't require me to have a colostomy bag. I did learn that a human has roughly sixty inches of colon, (large intestine), so losing 20 percent was tolerable. He was able to remove all the tumors, but he also removed twenty-four lymph nodes that could be carriers of the cancer. He sent those for testing and said the results would take a couple weeks to return. If any lymph nodes were infected, a PET (Positron-Emission Tomography) scan of my body would tell us if the cancer had spread. A PET scan is in simple terms, a color aided image to detect the spread of disease. More on that later. I still had to get my body back in shape to be discharged and sent home. Since I was cut open, I now had eleven staples in my stomach from the belly button on up. I was told recovery in the hospital would be a minimum of three days, and I needed to have a bowel movement to make sure things were working inside.

The next day was Saturday, and it was now one week since this all began. Today was the wonderful day that I realized I had a catheter in me. That's right, for the last twenty-four hours, I had been pissing through a tube and didn't even know or feel it! How can that be? Because in about five minutes, I sure was going to feel it come out. So in walks the nurse who casually says, "Okay Mr. Porter, it's time to take the catheter out." All I could think of was, "Excuse me. What?" Drugs are a wonderful thing for surgery, but once they wear off, things get a little more intense. So my first question to her was, "How will this feel?" She replied, "Oh you won't feel a thing." In my typical smart ass tone I said, "Really? Because that thing down there is not meant to have anything inside it?" Without further ado, as she removed the invading tube, as Cosmo Kramer once proclaimed on *Seinfeld*, I let the expletives fly! I mean seriously, this was not a fun ten seconds. In all my experiences over the past two years, this was the second most painful experience. The most painful was soon to follow.

By this time, I had some visitors arriving from time to time. My friend, Mike, just happened to be there when it was time to use the bathroom for the first time since the catheter came out. As I strolled gingerly to the bathroom, I said to him, "If you hear me scream, don't be alarmed." Let's just say some loud noise came from the bathroom, and of course Mike was outside trying not to laugh too hard. I thought about the time when I was around nine years old and I had sliced my foot open walking home barefoot from the swimming pool. My dad rushed me to the hospital to get the thing stitched up. Twenty-five stitches were required. The doctor stuck my open wound in a warm, soapy bowl of water. I thought that was bad. Wrong! This was worse. If there was ever a feeling of what it's like to piss vinegar, this was the feeling. Good news was that the discomfort went away after a few episodes. However, more fun was soon to come.

Now we move to Monday, December 18. This was hopefully the day I could go home, but I still didn't have a bowel movement. I was praying for one to come. What came was the opposite. I had hiccups so bad, and such bad heartburn developing, that I began to throw up. This was not good because I had eleven fresh staples in my gut. They had to get this reversed. So they gave me Thorazine to reverse the effects. Thorazine is an anti-psychotic drug, which is also used to relieve prolonged hiccups. By the next day I was feeling better. While it still took a while to do my "business", I was able to be sent home on Friday the 22nd. Now two weeks and twenty pounds lighter, I was heading home and in time for Christmas. An added bonus was turning fifty the day after Christmas. Not the way I envisioned it, but at least I was home alive and with my family. My family made it up to me as they had a fiftieth birthday celebration for both me and Colleen the following July.

After the holidays and the New Year, it was time to get my staples out. I also received word that three lymph nodes tested positive, and a PET scan was scheduled for January 8. The scan revealed a tumor in my liver. When I looked at the scan, it literally looked like I swallowed a Titleist golf ball and it came to rest smack dab in the middle of my liver. In golf terms, that was the shittiest lie I ever had, but you play it as it lies in golf, and in life. Perfectly round shape and totally bizarre to see. My oncologist and I mapped out the next nine months of what was needed. On January 18, I would have a CT Rated Infused Power Port implanted in my chest below the collar bone. This would serve as the access point for all my blood work, chemotherapy and contrast needed for scans. It's basically a round, rubber bulb called a septum. This is the access point for the needle. A small, plastic flexible tube called the catheter, (not the bad kind), connects to the septum and empties on the other end into the heart. I call this thing my lifeline, and to this day, it is still in me. Oncologists usually want you to wait a year of being cancer free before having it removed. This beats the hell out of them sticking needles in your arm every time.

This brings up the first of many times I will talk about music and how it played an important part of getting me through this fight. When I went to get the power port surgically implanted, they laid me down in a dimly lit room. The song playing in the room was, *The Rooster* by *Alice in Chains*. I thought this was a little strange but also really cool and soothing. It totally put my mind at ease and fifteen minutes later the power port was in. When I look in the mirror at this thing navigating across my upper chest, it amazes me once again how quick and precise these doctors are with their work.

I now had the entire weekend of January 19 to 21 to think about my first of twenty infused chemotherapy treatments. The first forty were coming to a close. These were the forty days since being told I had cancer. These were the forty days I had to prepare for my treatments. How long the treatments would last was anybody's guess.

Beginning January 22 and every two weeks after, I would go to the hospital to begin chemotherapy. Each cycle of chemo would last four to six cycles, and after those were complete, another scan would be ordered. Blood work (they call it labs) was the first step before every chemo session, and those results would then be sent over to the oncologist for review to approve the treatment. Five hours of chemotherapy would follow in the hospital. After that, they would connect a bag full of drugs into a pump, which attached to my port, and send me home for forty-six hours of continuous chemo.

Have you ever wondered what's in a "chemo cocktail?" Each patient's mix could be different, but currently, here is my "menu" this month. I can tell you this much. If the judges for the "Scripps National Spelling Bee" want to stump some teenagers, try some of these words on them. The first round of appetizers consists of pre-meds. A simple taste of 0.25mg of atropine, followed by 25mg of diphenhydramine, or in layman's terms, *Benadryl*. Keep in mind this stuff is all going directly into the veins, so the warning, "may cause drowsiness", hits you in like three minutes instead of 60. Then it's on to 10mg of dexamethasone (Decadron). Now we move on to the main course. 300mg of irinotecan (Camptosar), followed by a 250mcg injection of palonosetron, and 670mg of ramucirumab (Cyramza) in a sodium chloride drip. Last, and certainly not least, is the final course, dessert. I get to take that at home and enjoy it for two days. 4850mg of fluorouracil(Adrucil) pumping on a continuous basis for forty-six hours, and when that is completed, my wife plays nurse and disconnects me.

This is our life every two weeks. Not a life anyone in my family asked for, but it's OUR life. That's the way we have to look at it and accept it. The journey is real and we must believe our destination is a life without cancer.

A-T-T-I-T-U-D-E

DON'T WORRY, I'M NOT GOING TO BORE YOU BY GOING INTO detail about each of my treatments. All I will say is we are at forty-seven and counting. What I want to bring to light is how I approached the fight against cancer.

I begin with attitude because it was the most important aspect in starting on the path to beating cancer. I want to emphasize that many people with good and positive attitudes lose their fight with cancer. However, my point is it's better to attack positively than to look on the dark side of what you have in front of you. When you wake up every morning, you really only have one thing you can control, your ATTITUDE. Maybe you went to bed the night before unhappy with your spouse or child about something? Maybe a problem at work kept you restless or a dispute with a friend? On the flip side, maybe you went to bed happy, calm or stress free? Whatever the situation was or is, your attitude put you in that position and will take you on a path for what lies ahead each and every day. In fact, your attitude sets the tone in your life, because it's the only thing YOU can control. There is a quote by Charles R. Swindoll that states, "I am convinced that life is 10% what happens to me and 90% how I react to it". From the moment my wife took me to the Emergency Room on December 9, 2017, and for the three-plus years since, my attitude toward everything made this recovery possible. It wasn't the only thing, nor was it perfect every day, but it was the only thing I could control. What I've learned about the word, "control" is this. It's something most people want to possess but very few know how to manage. It's not easy. However, there is a way to make it easier, and it's when you accept these few things about control. It's your life, you can do what you want to do and say what you want to say, but with that comes feedback from others. If you aren't prepared for that feedback, whether positive or negative, then be very careful what you say and do, how you say and do it, and lastly, why? For every action is a reaction. In a nutshell, take care of yourself first. Control what you can. Remember, your way is not the way for everyone, so don't force it on anyone. The more flexible and adaptive you are, the more control you can have. Little by little I'm finding my way to a better me, but there are still bumps on the road I must travel over. I know I can be better, but can't we all?

Now back to attitude. When I break down the word, "Attitude", look at this way when addressing a situation in your life.

Ask. Is the issue you are experiencing worth your time? If it wasn't something you started or should be involved in, then move on. Many people become obsessed with how others perceive them. We have this desire to be liked by everyone, but in reality, that's not possible. It hurts us if others say or do things in a negative way behind our back. The older I've become, the more I've realized that's not a "me" problem. Your attitude will improve the more you distance yourself from the negativity in your life.

Think. Think before you act. Doing this will eliminate many problems before they develop.

Toughen Up. The tougher you are mentally, the better off you will be. Fighting cancer taught me one very important thing. The mind is tougher than the body.

Identify. By definition, identify means to recognize or distinguish something considered worthy of attention. Why fight something not worth anything to you? We all identify material things that have worth to us, like a car, house, jewelry, and clothes. Why not identify things that mentally bring us worth?

Truthful. Be honest with yourself with everything you do in life. Is what you are doing the right thing? Are you trying to be a good person? It's much easier to live with a positive attitude if you are doing positive things in your life on a regular basis. Nobody is perfect, but that doesn't mean we can't strive for perfection.

Understand. Whatever your attitude is at any given point of the day, understand the ramifications it could have on others around you. Any negativity you bring into a situation could have an impact on another person's day. That goes both ways too. Your positive mood or actions could also provide a better outlook to someone, who up until that moment, was not having a good day. A smile, hug, gesture or a simple "hello" goes a long way.

Demand. The road most travelled is boring. Demand more from yourself. Think of all the times you took the easy way out. Get yourself motivated to try harder. Try something new. You will be amazed how much better you might feel at the end of the day when you do.

Effort. Anything you want out of life requires effort. What you give is what you get. This is a dying mantra among many people today, especially young people. If it requires effort, it's just easier to quit. If you want easy, then sit on your butt. If you want to achieve something, then put in the effort. If you want to see real effort, go to a cancer hospital and sit in a POD where six people are having poisonous drugs put in their bodies and fighting for their lives. Look at the efforts of the nurses and doctors providing unending care to these patients. Their attitudes are amazing!

I have to work on my attitude every day. Everyone from my wife to my boss reminds me about it. I need to be better. However, I can say with all honesty, I put as much as I could since December 9, 2017, in my attitude to beat cancer. From the moment of diagnosis to the moment of hopefully becoming cancer free, it has been my mission to beat it. My hope for you is to find that positivity in your life to have a better attitude to accomplish whatever it is you want. Whether it's beating cancer or simply finding satisfaction in your life, a positive attitude instills the belief that we can accomplish anything.

Quick Hits

IF YOU REALLY WANT SOMETHING TO HAPPEN, YOU FIRST HAVE to believe it can happen. Wishing it might happen doesn't qualify. If you believe it can happen, then you have to go out and make it happen. One of the things you will find out after being diagnosed with cancer is how hospitals and doctors are so quick to put you in a bucket with others in your situation. As a Stage IV cancer patient, I was told there was an 11 percent chance of living five years. I immediately took that challenge to believe I could be that 11 percent. Unfortunately, most cancer patients look at the situation as there is no way they can survive. How can anyone overcome those odds?

You first must believe it can be done. Cancer can be beaten. More and more people are beating cancer each year. The beauty of a challenge is the belief that in the end you will have that chance to be a survivor. Make no mistake, if you are fighting cancer right now, it will be the toughest challenge of your life. However, each little victory is a step closer to your goal of being cancer free. It's that belief that makes the journey a little easier to navigate.

As we grow older, we tend to forget the joys we experienced in our youth. In particular, competing in sports. What was greater than hitting that game winning basket? Scoring the game winning goal? Making that five foot putt to win a golf match? Scoring that game winning touchdown? Even if you never experienced it, maybe you experienced it in your dreams? Or you played it out in the backyard? Is there anything funnier and more relatable than Bill Murray pretending to be the "Cinderella Story" at the *MASTERS* from the movie *Caddyshack*? If you haven't seen the movie, then find it on YouTube. Or Google, "Carl Spackler". I could go on with more analogies, but the point being we all should have a desire to compete. That's all cancer really is about. A competition between mind and body. The belief that you can accomplish anything you want. You hear all the time from successful business people, entertainers, athletes, doctors, teachers etc. You can do anything in life you set your mind on doing. There are no limits on what you can accomplish. Fighting cancer is no different. You can beat it. Believe that it's nothing more than a goal that you have set in your life and go out and score that winning goal. Be that 11 percent. Believe that you can do it and make it happen. You can't spell "believe" without L-I-V-E. Live every day.

I mentioned earlier that I'm a crier. When dealing with cancer, whether it's as a patient or caregiver, please know it is alright to cry. In fact, it's good for you as far as I'm concerned, and Jim Valvano thought so as well. Many times I found myself crying while driving my car. I do a lot of traveling in my vehicle, and there are many miles of windshield time I endure. I found these moments to be the best time to release my emotions. A song on the radio may trigger a cry. A thought about my wife or children, or, simply the thought of the unknown of my health. Cancer is a scary thing. I'm not naïve to that. You can't hold back the emotions. It's not healthy.

You will also experience the cry when receiving good news. Those are good cries when you receive news from the doctors or nurses that your blood levels are improving, or your CT scan showed tumors are shrinking. The result that will come from crying is it will release stress that you have. Stress is never a good thing, especially when you are dealing with cancer. The mind needs to be strong and focused as you battle your way through this. This is where courage really needs to come to the forefront. This goes for everyone involved in your support group. The moment you are diagnosed is the moment that courage needs to be switched on. Treatment days are where I found the most courage. I found that from the others in the treatment room (POD) with me. I was fortunate to always have someone with me. When it wasn't Colleen, it would be another family member like my parents or in-laws, or a friend. I was also fortunate enough to have friends who worked in the hospital where I was getting treatment. Whoever was with me, they always brought great conversation, support and FOOD! I loved the food. However, it never went unnoticed how there was always that one person in the POD who was alone. The one thing about me, good or bad, is my desire to ask questions. My wife thinks I ask too many dumb questions, or even rhetorical questions. Either way, I was genuinely interested in how others fighting this disease looked at their situation. I was always very careful to make sure not to pry too far into personal lives. There were times where my better judgment took over and would realize some people just wanted to be left alone. You have to respect that. However, talking with these people gave me tremendous hope and courage to keep fighting. Some of these patients were far worse off than me. Those that were alone made me wonder, why? And there was always the time when I never saw them again. I had to just hope they were doing well.

One of these such moments was March 5, 2018. This was a treatment day, and I was feeling good. The oncologist told me my CEA marker, (Carcinoembryonic Antigen), had dropped. This was one marker they look at to see if the treatment is working. My weight was holding steady as well at 173. The day continued on as planned. One of the goals each patient has is to ring the bell on the seventh floor. Each patient who completes their treatments rings that bell. It signifies the beginning of the healing process. It's a very significant time in a cancer patient's life. I looked at that bell every time I was there, and I looked forward to ringing it with great enthusiasm. Two people rang the bell that day as applause was heard all over the floor. No matter what you were doing, or who you are, everyone stops and applauds.

However, not all days continue to be so rosy. Sometimes in treatment, the experience can become one of concern, sadness and sometimes just a little angered. On this day, as I sat in my POD receiving treatment, a young man was brought in and laid next to me in a bed. It was obvious he was in discomfort, so at first I left him alone. However, as the day went on and it was just the two of us left in the room, we exchanged a few words. We each introduced ourselves. His name was Ben and he was just thirty-one years old. This kid still had a lifetime ahead of him, but he knew his time was short. All I said to him before I left was, "You are a brave young man. Don't give up. Don't ever give up." Ben replied, "Jimmy V." I damn near lost it and had to say goodbye before I broke down in tears. That was the first and last time I ever saw Ben.

Life has a funny way of showing you hope in the middle of a situation that seems so desperate. While I watched others come and go during my three-plus years of treatment, it made me realize that one important thing. I was still coming, which meant I was still alive. All these patients I crossed paths with, whether they knew it or not, passed along their strength to me to keep fighting. I said that I'm a crier, and right now as I type this, I'm crying. Whenever I feel weakness or fear to do something, I always find myself thinking back to my days sitting in my treatment chair with a warm blanket on me. I soon realize nothing in life is too tough to tackle head on. For whatever lies ahead of me can't be as bad as what I left behind.

Lastly, one of the most frustrating side effects of chemotherapy is what cancer patient's call, "chemo brain." While my long-term memory remains intact, it is the short-term memory that occasionally causes me problems. Not only that, but sometimes I will experience confusion, trouble concentrating, and many times just trying to find the right word in a conversation. Just the other day I was getting gas in my car and I went inside to buy a lottery ticket. As hard as I tried, I couldn't say the word, "Powerball", to the cashier. Thankfully the young lady figured out what I was trying to say.

There is research being done to understand the memory changes that affect people with cancer. I've never sat down and discussed this with a doctor or anyone else with cancer. I don't find it to be a huge burden because I have worked throughout my chemotherapy, and nobody has ever mentioned to me that it's a problem. I'm in sales, so I do take a lot of notes, and when I'm on my laptop, I keep a pen and paper next to me and write down ideas so I don't forget them. My wife tells me at times that I ask the same questions more than once, or she tells me something five minutes ago that I have forgotten. That could also just be a lack of attention, which is another side effect of chemo brain.

My hope is, that in time, this will go away. Then again, someone may have to inform me. I might forget.

Riding the
Storm Out

THREE MONTHS BEFORE I WAS DIAGNOSED WITH CANCER, I rode in my first PEDAL THE CAUSE charity bicycle ride. The ironic thing was, I had cancer and didn't even know it. After I was diagnosed and all my lab work was tested, the oncologist told me I was likely carrying this with me for over a year. My friend, Mike Christian, is on the Board for this charity. His father, John Christian, Sr., battled cancer for twenty-five years, and his entire family is involved with this. He is one of the main reasons I ride. In 2016, I showed up to watch and cheer them on. So I want to relay a quick story about Mr. and Mrs. Christian. I've known the Christian family since they moved to St. Louis when I was in the sixth grade. In the beginning, Mrs. Christian was not my biggest fan. In her defense, I was the kid always in trouble or looking for trouble. I was that kid that stirred up shit, so Mrs. Christian gave me tough love. Today, I have the utmost love and respect for her. More importantly was the strength, inspiration and determination her husband has given me in my battle with cancer. Unfortunately, Mr. Christian is not with us physically, but his spirit lives on in so many people's lives, including mine. When I got my diagnosis and began my chemotherapy, Mrs. Christian sent me a poem by Paula Vlahovich. It went like this:

> "Reach out to find what makes you strong. As you walk the
> road, it widens—your family, friends and caregivers are with
> you and their love will light the way. You can walk with hope

now, and you are learning what will come and how to face it—making choices, finding ways to cope. These times can show you the courage that's within. Hold out your hands to others who walk the road with you, for you have the energy and healing light to share. Godspeed to all who come this way, and those who walk beside. Cancer can't crush the power of your love."

In 2017, I decided to sign up and ride, and I'm glad I made that decision. I'm not even an avid bike rider. In fact, I don't even own a bike. I ride one time a year, and it's in this event the last Sunday of September. I appreciate and believe in this cause so much, that I rent a bike and ride twenty miles. The last three years, I rode while still receiving infused chemo treatments. I made sure to schedule my treatments around the event. I didn't want to be hooked up to anything and too weak to ride.

PEDAL THE CAUSE is, in my opinion, the premier fund raiser in the state of Missouri. The story behind it and what they have accomplished is incredible. It was founded in 2009 by two-time lymphoma survivor Bill Koman. Like me, he received his treatment from the *Siteman Cancer Center in St. Louis*. After beating cancer the second time, Mr. Koman wanted to give back to *Siteman*, so he initiated the *Cancer Frontier Fund*, now known as the *Siteman Investment Program*. This is a project that awards grant money to cancer research to the *Washington University School of Medicine* physicians. He then went one step further and that's when PEDAL THE CAUSE was formed. This project guarantees 100 percent of all funds raised would stay in St. Louis. Those funds go to fund research at *Siteman Cancer Center and Siteman Kids St. Louis Children's Hospital*.

Since 2009, PEDAL THE CAUSE has raised almost $30M for cancer research. 2019 was the biggest year ever, as almost 3800 riders raised over $4.7M. Even with Covid-19 in 2020, we were able to raise over $3M. Out of 3500 riders, I was able to finish in the top fifty of fundraising with a total of $7,270. This is an event that has a huge impact on the local economy. TASTE THE CAUSE takes place on Saturday. Numerous restaurants and beverage suppliers have a celebration for the riders and survivors. There is a "Living Proof" ceremony Saturday night with guest speakers who have survived their cancer battles, and all battlers and survivors are introduced in the amphitheater setting. This is a weekend that celebrates life, and the cause is to never quit until we live in a world without cancer.

Pedal the Cause 2019

To fully understand what PEDAL THE CAUSE is all about, you really must experience it in person. Like I said, it is always the last weekend in September. It is held in the West St. Louis suburb of Chesterfield, Missouri. If you have never experienced it, I highly suggest doing so. You can ride, volunteer or simply come out and enjoy the atmosphere and cheer on the thousands of men, women and children riding for a cause. It is the most professionally run event I've seen, and I've participated in and attended many events, and I'm not just talking about charity events. They are fully staffed year round, and the work never stops. If you would like to learn more about it, please visit (www.pedalthecause.org). I personally want to thank my team, TEAM KEELEY, for bringing me on board. It's an honor to ride with each and every one of you.

Entre Nous

I'M A BELIEVER THAT MUSIC PLAYS A BIG ROLE IN LIFE, AT LEAST it does in my life. My friends poke fun at me because I know quite a bit about music, yet I never really collected or owned albums, tapes, compact discs, or have some huge playlist on my phone. One thing that got me through my fight with cancer was listening to music, in particular, the band RUSH. This is a three man band that played for forty years. Known as a "progressive-metal" band, they were often referred to as, "musical nerds." Their skills were second to none, but it was their lyrics that made them, in my opinion, brilliant. The main man behind those lyrics was their drummer, Neil Peart. Not only was he arguably the best drummer to ever play, but his intellect was incredible. One of the songs he wrote, that really resonated with me during my cancer, was "ENTRE NOUS", French for, "And between Us." There are many ideas about the song's meaning. Whether it was about a connection between two people, a group of people, or the universe in general? It was also thought that Peart wrote it about his connection between him and the audience he played in front of during concerts. No matter what it's about, I listen to songs and find the meanings they have in my life. I think many of us do. As I am now fifty-three years old, I can hear a song on the radio that was released in 1986, and immediately I relate that to a time in my life when I first heard it. I remember Jim Quist coming to my house and having me get in his car to listen to the new WHITESNAKE album. John Cougar's *Jack & Diane*, taking me back to eighth grade and parties in Jeff Wissel's basement. *Shook Me All Night Long* at Molly O'Neal's house. And *Keep on Loving You* at David Rogers' eighth grade, co-ed parties. But to this day, and likely always, the best music memories were always in Dan McNamara's basement we called, *Smoke N Mirrors*. There have been three, since Dan has now owned three houses since he moved back to St. Louis in 2006. While I'll always cherish Mike Christian doing his best Mike Reno (Lead singer of LOVERBOY) impressions, nights at *Smoke N Mirrors I, II, and III* always ended with a RUSH song or video. Even though RUSH retired five years ago, and unfortunately the passing of Neil Peart on January 7, 2020 to brain cancer, they will always hold the number one place in my heart for music. As I've digressed now, let me get back to my story about *Entre Nous* and cancer.

I took on the cancer as a personal battle between me and "it." In order to beat your enemy you need to know your enemy. I knew nothing about cancer before 2017, other than it was a terrible disease that had taken many people I knew and loved away from me. Even the greatest doctors and scientists in the world are still trying to learn how cancer navigates our bodies. If we had all the answers, we would have cures for all cancer. At least this is how I look at it. So when I listen to the words of the song, *Entre Nous*, I get this connection, right or wrong, the relationship I had with cancer. From the very beginning of the song, "We are secrets to each other, each one's life a novel no one else has read." Cancer victims all wonder, "How did I get cancer?" I asked my doctors and they can't pin point how or why I got cancer. As I stated before, you can drive yourself crazy thinking about the why, where, when and how. But I stated earlier about my time working at the dry cleaning store and a story about it. I used to clean out the machine that dry cleaned the clothes. It used a highly carcinogenic solvent called "perchloroethylene (perc)". Even though I wore protection, I can only guess this is what may have been the cause of my cancer. I really don't know? Anyway, on with the story.

The song moves on with, "We're linked to one another by such slender threads." This particular line takes me back to when the oncologist asked me when the last time was I went to see a doctor for a physical. I told her, "at least 25 years." She said, "This could have likely been prevented with annual check-ups and blood work." That truly hit home with me as something that simple could have kept me from all this. That decision not to go see a doctor likely was the "slender thread" linking me to cancer.

As the song weaves on, the line of, "Each of us a world apart, alone and yet together like two passing ships." Cancer was living and growing in my body without my knowledge. I had no symptoms telling me to get checked out. It was only a matter of time before our worlds would meet and become one. I like to say that when I met cancer, I realized the only thing I "knew" about it was there was nothing to like. There were no conversations we had. It was always me talking and it listening. The more I told it to die, the better I felt. Between us, I knew that I had more ammunition in my corner than it did. For I wasn't fighting alone. I had a TEAM with me, and it couldn't overcome the overwhelming power of TEAM PORTER.

Then the words come out that take me into my treatment and how to look at cancer. "We are Islands to each other, building hopeful bridges on a troubled sea. Some are burned or swept away, some we would not choose but we're not always free." I never even told my wife these things I was dealing with on a daily basis. She knew I was on my phone a lot with headphones on looking for songs on *You Tube*. Late nights sitting up listening to music to carry me through without worrying my family. At times I felt stranded on an island trying to reach a destination. The destination was being cancer free, and my only goal was to get off that island that I didn't choose to be on.

In closing on this song, the chorus is what I take away from it moving forward in life. This is where I learned how I wanted to treat others moving forward. It's like my final ACT in life. These words can be used in any relationship you are in, whether it's a marriage, friendship, with a family member, and even in politics.

"Just between us, I think it's time for us to recognize the differences we sometimes feared to show. Just between us, I think it's time for us to realize the spaces in between…leave room…for you and I to grow."

Now you know a little more about the trio from Canada and their influence on my life. As I've aged, I try to listen to music I didn't like before. While I still find some of it difficult to stomach, it always helps to just listen to the words. You just might find some meaning in a song to get you through a difficult time in your life. I tell people who don't like RUSH this exact thing. And just between us, I've liked Engelbert Humperdinck for a long time now. I'm not sure I've ever told anyone that?

The New Normal,
Or Is It?

THIS WAS THE TOUGHEST TOPIC TO WRITE ABOUT, BECAUSE many cancer patients use the term "new normal". As I write this, our country is smack dab in the middle of the COVID-19 pandemic. That now has people using the term "new normal". So, my opinions are just that, and I'm not here to offend anyone for using the words "new normal".

Before I got cancer, I don't recall hearing much about these two words. I always knew it as some bad sit-com on television or a shortened version of the twin city with Bloomington in Illinois. However, for the last three-plus years, I hear and read about it everywhere. Everyone has their own way of dealing with things, but I never found my life to be real normal in the first place. Hell, you read in the beginning of this book how crazy the first twenty-seven years of my life were. So, how would I know what to call my, "new normal"?

I never found it normal to have a power port implanted in my chest. I didn't find it normal to have forty-seven rounds of chemotherapy and counting, five rounds of radiation or three surgeries. Was it normal not to shower for three days in a row? If you didn't know, I can't shower while my power port is accessed. I was also told it wasn't normal for a Stage IV cancer patient to never get nausea or lose his hair with the drugs I was receiving. There was nothing normal about me as I fought this, but then again, you could ask a lot of people that know me that I wasn't real "normal" before I got cancer either.

I've been trying to find the best way to explain what the "new normal" means to me, because it's not in me to try and figure out what it means to you.

My new normal is to just get up each day and live like nothing happened. I truly mean that. I don't want to be defined by cancer. I don't want people to just remember me as the guy who beat cancer. I would like to think I'm remembered as a good husband, father, son, brother, uncle and friend. I continue to work on that, and at times, I fail. I know cancer will always be a part of my life, but when you break it down, it's only been with me approximately 6 percent of my life. I've been dealing with it for 37 of the 637 months I've been alive.

I know some would argue this point with me, and I can understand their side of it. Yes, it's possible to say that my last "normal" day was December 8, 2017. My "new normal" took over December 9, 2017 and hasn't ended. Now that I'm back in treatment again after a short hiatus, does it mean I'm on my "new normal Part II?" Is the COVID-19 pandemic another "new normal" for me? Others may argue my "new normal" is still going on because I have follow up scans and blood work to get every ten to twelve weeks, but not one time was any of those days the same. None of my treatment days went the same. They all had different things that happened to me, whether it was a longer wait, different nurse, bad news, good news etc. Those days changed my life forever, and by that, it opened my eyes to see things in an entirely different way. When I look back on my life, the only constant thing I've done is go to sleep at night and wake up every morning. I don't get up every day and do the same things I did when I was six, sixteen, twenty-six, thirty-six or forty-six. THAT would NOT be normal.

Some words that describe normal are: conforming, usual, typical or expected. Is that how you want to describe your life? Not me. I've thought about this and I'm going to call this second stage of my life as the "new different." There's that word again, different. That's really what all of our lives are on a daily basis. We may do some of the same things like eat, work, and play, but we do them in different ways. Why? Because all of us are different. The situations we are in and the people around us are different. Different is not the same. Unlike in nature, form or quality. Different is distinct and separate. That's what makes us who we are, the fact that we are all different. We adapt and survive.

So I challenge you to try different things. What have you done different in your life since the COVID-19 pandemic came into your life? I know you aren't likely attending sporting events, concerts, going to the theater, dining out, or going to school or possibly, and unfortunately, working. You are likely watching too much crap the media is spinning twenty-four hours a day online, television, radio and print. I hope you're doing things different than before. Maybe you have picked up a new hobby like cooking, baking, golf, tennis or sewing? Cherish these weeks, and now months, you've had to get to know your family again. Realize that work isn't everything in life. Don't slide back into your norm when we do get back to socializing again, because in time, the so called "new normal" will change again. Kick start that new different in your life. Whether that's to start a business you never thought you could, or something as simple as eating a food you thought you never liked. In my life it started with this, and that's writing a book, that as little as two years ago, I never imagined doing.

My Inspiration

ANOTHER PERSON IN MY THOUGHTS AS I WRITE THIS BOOK was a man named Brian Froneyberger. Brian lost his three year battle on October 3, 2018. Brian was forty-six years young. He left behind a beautiful wife, Donna, and two wonderful kids, Gage and Madi. The story of Brian became a local feel good story of courage, love and the bonding of an entire community. Local TV stations covered his last month of life on a regular basis. His son is a very good friend of my oldest son, Drew. The Fort Zumwalt West High school football team, the West High Middle School, and Brian, brought the community together like I've never seen before. Parents, teachers, students, friends, and strangers rallied around Brian hoping he could fight to live that next day. Courageously, Brian would still attend the football games for his son, and he attended games that his daughter cheered for in the 8th grade. Their kids and their friends were at the hospice center during his last days. They were there almost every day, and one by one they each said their goodbyes to him in private. Brian's father said it was the most unbelievable display of kindness and love he has ever seen from such a young group of people. The high school student body, almost 2000 strong, united like nothing ever before. During homecoming week, the students sat in unity, in a heart shaped circle on the football field, and sat in memory of Brian for forty-six minutes. One minute for each year of his life. In a fitting end to the homecoming festivities, Gage and his girlfriend were named Homecoming King and Queen. Brian's strong will to live, love, and his never ending interest in his children and their friends will never be forgotten. People attracted to Brian because he was so unselfish and had such a concern for others. He was a father, husband, son, coach, friend, and most importantly, a guy who knew how to LIVE his life to the fullest every day of the week. Donations from complete strangers were pouring into his GO FUND ME page because his story reached thousands of people across the region.

Brian is an example of why I won't let my cancer be a negative influence on me or anyone around me. Our families went on a weekend trip five years ago, and Brian was diagnosed with neck and head cancer one month later. I watched him battle with great positive energy, and when I was diagnosed over two years later, there was Brian and Donna at our house showing their support and asking how they could help. I didn't know it at the time, because Brian wasn't one to worry others with his problems, but he had already been informed his cancer was terminal. He fought to the end. Through his fight, he showed an entire school of teenagers and adults, how to live, how to love, and how to face adversity head on. How life was a daily grind of twists and turns, but a positive view on them will get you through to the next day. I will never understand why any of this happened to Brian, but I do know his loss made others stronger and better people.

In closing, remember that life is short. Hug your kids. Kiss your spouse or significant other every day like it's the last kiss you will ever have. Make family your priority, not your work. Be there when a family member or friend needs help. Reach out, help out, and get out there and make a difference in your community. Be a coach. A mentor. A volunteer. A Leader. Remember, Life is not measured by the number of breaths we take, but the number of moments that take our breath away.

Brothers

AT THIS POINT IN TIME, I WAS IN THE MIDDLE OF ANOTHER twelve rounds of chemo to fight off the cancer that had now spread to my lungs. But on this day, that was all forgotten and was truly a day that took my breath away. It was an evening I will never forget because of the unselfish and true friendship exhibited by eleven guys. Chree, JMAC, Strubey, Big O, Ned, Crazy, Sauce, Maloney (Loner), Doc, DMAC and Condor. Like many who were in my corner praying, helping and supporting me and my family, these guys pulled the surprise of the decade on me. We all got together to watch the Blues/Stars playoff hockey game at a local establishment. You will need to know a quick preview of my golf life for this to make sense. As I stated earlier, I attempted to play professional golf early in my life. Attempted the very key word here. After I gave it up, I just continued to play golf with my 1992 edition, Ping Eye irons. Not to mention, a hodgepodge of drivers and putters from the pre-Tiger era. It became a laughing point every time some of us played golf. And here it was, 2019, and I was still hacking it around with twenty-seven-year-old clubs.

Now on with the story. We had just sat down to order drinks when these guys hand me a couple of envelopes. I proceeded to open the first one which had a card, with a handwritten poem and gift card. The poem went as follows: "Hold your fire, keep it burning bright. Hold the flame 'til the dream ignites. A Spirit with a vision is a dream with a mission. You can fight without ever winning, but never ever win without a fight." - Love, Your Friends.

It took a lot for me to read that out loud, and I was so blown away that I didn't take much notice to the gift card. They had to remind me to look at the back of it. As if the card wasn't enough, these guys pitched in and bought me a gift card with a $1400 value to a local golf shop so I could buy new golf clubs, shoes and a bag. Or, whatever I felt I needed. On top of that, there was another envelope full of free golf certificates for roughly twenty rounds of golf to a local course.

It was like they could sense I was in need of this. I hadn't picked up a golf club in over eighteen months. They wanted me out there playing and were there to make that happen. I never doubted who my true friends were, but this, along with many other instances of random acts of kindness, solidified my belief in that saying above. This took my breath away.

Description: Just a few of my lifelong friends who have supported me.
L to R: Mike Connelly, John McMahon, Tim McWay, Mike Christian,
Dave Krobath, Dan McNamara, Tim Bohr. Kneeling: Me

Pump It... Off!

I WAS TOLD MY TREATMENTS MIGHT BE DIFFICULT, AND AFTER number fourteen, everything was going along smoothly. The pump I carried around in a bag that looked like a purse was a little awkward. It had roughly a three foot plastic tube that would unravel out of the bag and hang around my right leg. The reason for this was I was too dumb to realize this bag could actually strap around my waist. Then again, maybe they told me and I was just too lazy to strap it on? I continued to carry this over my shoulder and let it hang by my side. Whenever I would get dressed, I had to be very careful to put the bag down and not step on the tube. The tube was attached to a needle, which was inserted in my port, which was inside my chest. The most important thing to remember about this pump and port combo is the drug running through the tube into the body. It is toxic and can cause a slight burn or rash if it hits the skin. After approximately fifty hours of treatment, it will take forty-eight to seventy-two hours to release from my body. Needless to say, I was told, should the port needle ever become disconnected from my body, it is imperative to close off the flow of drugs and get to the hospital as soon as possible.

I was home alone and decided to take a bath. I still had to be careful with the pump and not drop it in the bathtub. I enjoyed the occasional free time of relaxing and listening to music. All was going as planned until I started to get dressed. Going on seven months of chemo at this time, neuropathy was getting pretty bad. Neuropathy causes tingling and numbness in your hands and feet, so it can be difficult to keep your balance. Think of a time when you got drunk one night and tried to take off your clothes so you could get in your bed. Now imagine that in reverse. All was going well until I tried to put on my pants. Left leg in, check. Right leg lifted, I began to fall to the left. I tried balancing myself by thrusting my right leg down the pant leg. One big problem. My foot snagged the tube, and the force of my weight ripped the tube and needle out of my chest.

I looked down and saw blood on my chest. The needle had been ripped out, and the only thing between me and the chemo flowing freely is the tape holding it down. I immediately reached down and clamped the tube closest to the pump. I had to get to the hospital quickly, but first I needed to finish getting dressed without causing any more damage. The one good thing was I didn't have to put an undershirt on, because I knew that was only coming off as soon as I reached the hospital. I slipped on a button down oxford, slipped on some loafers, and high tailed it for the car.

The first time I drove to a hospital with such urgency was thirteen years earlier when Colleen went into labor with our son, Grant. As I pulled up to the E.R. entrance that day, her water broke. Our new car, purchased three days earlier, was now christened. Thankfully, the car had high end, faux leather seats, it was cold, and she was wearing a knee length overcoat. This time, I was actually hoping for a police car to chase me as I was weaving through traffic and doing 60 in a 35. I was having flashbacks from high school. I always wondered what it would be like to have a cop chase me, knowing I could break every speed limit in a two city radius without consequences. It never happened, but I did make it to the hospital with no accidents.

As I walked into Siteman Cancer Center in St. Peters, my craziness turned to calmness almost immediately. Yes, they were concerned, and they did wonder how the heck I drove myself to the facility, but the needle and drugs were contained, and they disconnected and re-connected my pump. Once I told them how it happened, they were laughing at me. Not laughing with me, but laughing at me. I only wish all this was on video. The video would be a YouTube sensation.

Ringin the Bell...
But Now What?

THE DAY CAME THAT I WAS LOOKING FORWARD TO, AND THAT was ringing the bell at SITEMAN. After twenty infused, chemo treatments, my liver was officially cancer free. The doctors and nurses informed me I could ring the bell because my treatments were over for now. Even though two spots on my lung were still there, they had not gotten any larger. I would continue with a maintenance plan of pills and monthly checkups.

Fast forward about thirty days. After returning home from my first maintenance checkup, I started to experience more stomach pain. I was just told all was still good with my scan and blood work, so I didn't think too much about it. However, after about five hours of it being more than discomfort, I had my wife take me to the E.R. We spent the next ten hours in the E.R., and all they could conclude was some blockage must be somewhere in my bowels. They admitted me to the hospital and took me off food and water for the next two days to see if it would "loosen" anything. Nothing got better. Now it was time for the dreaded barium sulfate experience. This is a contrast agent that you drink that allows scans to be seen more clearly. Every fifteen minutes, for ninety minutes, I had to drink this foul tasting shit. Each time between doses the staff would take another scan of my torso.

The next day the surgeon came in with the results, and it was concluded my lower intestine had become "twisted" in his words, and this was causing the pain. Five hours later, I was back in surgery. This time they were able to do the laparoscopic surgery of three incisions and send a scope in to fix the issue. The surgeon also explained to me how the lower intestine "floats" around inside you. That seems a little bizarre to me. However, another side effect from this type of surgery is where all the excess gas from the tube they snaked down my throat went. It releases through the diaphragm and into the phrenic nerve of the shoulder. Imagine someone delivering a direct blow on the A/C joint of your shoulder. If you've ever played football and experienced a "stinger", this is what it felt like. Thirty hours later I was released from the hospital. One year to the day of being told I had cancer, I was now back home again recovering.

Now the fun really begins. A week after surgery, I went back to see my oncologist. This is when the shit hit the fan. My first two surgeries were performed at a different hospital than where I received treatment. It never dawned on me to tell my oncologist that I went in for surgery, so she had no idea what happened the week before. She informed me that the drugs I was on and having surgery could have made me really sick. Sick? All I could think of was what do you call these last twelve months? A vacation? Anyway, I got the point, but didn't understand why the hospital didn't ask me anything about medication I was on before admitting me for surgery? So I was taken off medication for three weeks and told to come back after the first of the year.

When I did go back, things were getting a little worse in the blood work but nothing to worry about right now. However, when February rolled around, my CT scan revealed the spots on my lung were getting bigger. One that was particularly concerning because of the "irregular borders." A PET scan was being called in to see if the spotlights up and is an active cancerous cell. After fun with the insurance company delaying the PET scan, I finally had one that revealed cancerous nodules on my lung. In medical terms, the brightness scale is also known as, STANDARDIZED UPTAKE VALUES. The scale is 0 to 15. Anything more than three is considered to be cancerous. My spot lit up at 6.9. While all this was being presented to me, I decided it was time to switch oncologists. There were numerous factors that went into this decision, like lack of communication and my current hours and days I could go for treatment, so I deemed it best to move on. I stayed in the same network, but moved everything to another one of their locations and changed days from Monday to Friday for doctor and treatment visits. The next six months would be anything but ideal. If you are reading this and have any type of illness, I highly recommend at least two doctor opinions.

Houston,
We Have a Problem

SO NOW WITH THE CANCER IN MY LUNGS, I WAS ON A WAITING list for an immunotherapy trial and a third generation Avastin trial, ADT68A. However, I didn't qualify for either of those, so infused chemo would start back up again. It was these next six months where my instincts took over telling me something just wasn't right. Each and every time I completed a treatment, and leading up to the next one, nothing felt like it was working. Blood work would come back with mixed reviews. Scans would show three tumors, with one growing and the other two not. Or, the next scan showed two growing and one shrinking. Surgery was mentioned, but they never wanted to pull the trigger on it for various reasons. Either it was too risky, as one was too close to my diaphragm, or the tumor wasn't large enough. Then in mid-June of 2019, I got the sickest I've been since all this began.

My weight dropped to 150 as I was having all kinds of problems keeping water and food in me. I wasn't even trying to eat anymore. I called the doctor who asked exactly what was going on. I said, "Doc, within five minutes of eating or drinking anything, I'm sitting on the toilet like I'm getting ready for a colonoscopy, and this has been going on for almost three days now." He immediately responded with, "How quick can you get down to the hospital?" I'll let you know that without traffic, it's about a thirty-five minute drive from my house, so I replied, "in about 20 minutes." If I still had my trusty, green 1971 Maverick, I could have made it in fifteen. From the time I hung up the phone, they had me admitted and in a room within an hour. This was on a Monday, and by the next morning, I dropped five pounds to 145. Not to be too gross, but I had to excrete anything and everything from my body for testing. They were wanting to find out if I had a bacteria called, "Clostridium Difficile" or "C-Diff" for short, developing in my colon. After a shot in my gut and a handful of pills, the tests came back negative. Thankfully, by the time I checked out Tuesday late afternoon, I was at the *Village Bar* eating cheeseburgers with Chree, JMAC and Strubey. Nothing was ever officially diagnosed as to why this happened, and it was at this time I fully believed the chemo was doing nothing. It was just floating through my body killing nothing, but I let this go on for almost three more months. I let them continue the treatments because the cycle had to be completed.

A month later I was up to 157. Two weeks after that, I climbed to 164. And by the time I completed the chemo cycle on September 8, I weighed 172. PEDAL THE CAUSE was in three weeks, I felt strong, and my body felt strong. I went back for a follow up CT scan on the 13th, and the results gave us bad news. The tumors had grown by 20 percent. I met with a thoracic surgeon on the 19th, and he recommended a VIDEO ASSISTED THORACIC SURGERY (VATS) and it would only be a wedge resection, because the tumor was on the wall of my left lung, and it could easily be cut out and the surgery would be minimal. Three to four small incisions would be made, and each incision had a scope to do a particular job. Camera, light, cut, bag. The other main tumor was too far in the lung, and they wanted to hold off for now on that. The good news was that I needed to be off chemo for four weeks before any surgery could be performed, so riding in PEDAL THE CAUSE was going to happen. Surgery would wait until October 16, but I couldn't have the surgery until my lungs were deemed strong enough, and that required a lung function test. If nothing else, this was a very educational experience. I smoked for twenty-eight years, so I was curious to learn more about my lungs. Quick story on my smoking, as I don't recommend this for trying to quit smoking, but I had tried everything else, so I was desperate. I had promised my wife for years I would quit. First it was when we got married. Then it was when we had our first child. It went on and on until my nine-year-old daughter was walking around the house pretending to smoke. I never smoked in the house, and I always tried not to do it around my children. Obviously, that was an epic fail. So it was a nice night on April and the St. Louis Cardinals baseball game was on that night. I went out on my driveway with a radio, two packs of Marlboro Lights, a twelve-pack of

Busch beer and listened to the entire game. I smoked all forty cigarettes and drank all twelve beers. The next morning I was so sick that just the smell of a cigarette would have made me nauseous. I haven't smoked a cigarette since. That was April 19, 2012. Once again, mind over body. Smoking is an oral fixation more than anything. I hate to be a hypocrite and tell you to quit...but freaking quit if you are a smoker. That goes for the vaping too. It was one of the best decisions I ever made.

The lung function test was pretty hard. They put me in a small chamber where I would sit down and perform numerous inhaling and exhaling procedures to the point when I had no more air to blow. Fifteen seconds here, then twenty seconds, and on and on it went with little to no breaks between. All in all it lasted about forty-five minutes, and I came out with very positive results. So good that not only was I surprised, but so was the technician giving me the test. I graded out 12 percent higher than other men my age. Did I get an award? No. A lollipop? No. I got a ticket to have lung surgery, as I was healthy enough for that.

With close to three weeks now until surgery, it allowed me to start planning on where I would go for a second opinion. My instincts told me it was time to do that. These last rounds of chemo were just not going well, and now that surgery was an option, I needed to act fast. My sister, Julie, had a friend who had a connection at MD ANDERSON in Houston. Within a few days, I was on the phone talking to an oncologist and had my scans and surgery recommendation sent to them. They did agree that the re-section was the correct course of action, but other things on my charts had them concerned, so they wanted me down there for a few days of testing.

So two weeks after my surgery I was on a plane to Houston. This was a great trip. This was also another prime example of my support group really helping out. I had friends offering free airfare and extending offers to help in any way they could. Thank you, Jim Gloriod, DMAC and Dan Walsh for the assistance. My sister flew down from Milwaukee and met me. Her friend, Chris, who happens to be a pilot, has a condo in Houston where we stayed for three days. Jay Janik, an old high school classmate drove down from Austin with his wife and took me out for a lovely dinner, and an old grade school friend, Steve Sandweg, picked me up on my way out of town and took me to lunch and the airport. All these people really made the trip more comfortable for me. Lean on your friends and family.

More importantly, the real work that was done at the hospital put my mind at ease. I was told by the doctors that for the last three or four months, the chemo was doing nothing. It had run its course that far back. My instincts were dead on. However, I wasn't out of danger completely. The scan taken here did show the surgery went well, but now the tumor in the upper, middle area of the left lung had doubled in size. They said there was two options. 1) Surgery. 2) Targeted Radiation. They were going to send their report back to St. Louis to the thoracic surgeon for his recommendation of which option was best. So when I got back home, we met with the surgeon who thought surgery was too much, as it would require a complete lobectomy. So, he put me in touch with a radiation oncologist, Dr. Clifford Robinson.

The education continued as there is more prep work before they just start shooting lasers in your body to burn cancer cells. Since this would be targeted radiation, it would require 3D imaging and mapping of my lung. This was a very precise procedure known as STEREOTACTIC BODY RADIATION THERAPY. I would need five treatments in a seven-day span each time laying completely still for ten minutes. In order to do that, they had to build a body cast for me to lay in. I went in for a thirty-minute process that required me to lay on my back, on a table, with my arms crossed over my head without moving. They built this mold around me as I laid there. By the time they were done, my arms felt like bricks were attached to them. I could barely move them. Anyway, once that was done, that's the mold I would lay in for the treatments, and I would have a belt strapped tight across my waist to keep me from any heavy breathing, arms over my head, and feet tied together. All this took place Christmas week. I came in each morning, laid on my back again, while a fancy piece of equipment pinpointed lasers directly on the tumor in my lung. The best part was getting to pick the music while this went on for five days. I picked RUSH every day. Big shocker!

What Can I Do?

WHAT I WILL GET INTO NOW IS A DELICATE SUBJECT FOR SOME people who get sick as well as those who want to help. For me, this was never an issue. I'm fairly tolerant and understanding of what my friends and family were trying to do for me, my wife and children. However, on social media and a Facebook group I joined, other cancer patients really got bent out of shape when people asked them, "What can I do for you?" Or, "If you need anything, let me know?"

When you take those questions out of the context of someone fighting a life and death disease, they are very polite questions, and that is why they shouldn't be taken out of context. The intent of wanting to help is still there. The issue at hand is, people who aren't sick don't know what to do or how to help? It's not their fault. In all likelihood, they are just as scared for you and your family as you might be? I don't think most people are wired to ask for help, sympathy, pity, charity or whatever you may want to think it is. Nobody likes to feel helpless, but as I learned, this support is what we needed as a family. After a while, when people asked if I needed anything, I would tell them. Put yourself in the position of a friend wanting to do something for you and you shutting them down. Now you've laid a possible guilty feeling on them. As helpless as you feel as the sick patient, they feel just as bad not being able to support you.

I will walk you through how we handled things to make it easier for my support group to help my family, which in turn made it more comfortable for everyone. This may not be for everyone, but it's what I know. I decided it would be best to just be open with my disease. From the very start, it just made sense because it's who I am. The more information you relay to your friends and family, the fewer questions you will have. So almost immediately, my family knew we would need financial help. Colleen and I were a little uncomfortable about this, but my sister, Regan, took it upon herself to start a GO FUND ME page for us. We were blown away by the donations from people everywhere. Since I had to take about eight total weeks off work and only collect short term disability, the donations really helped.

Next, set up a social media page to update your progress. I used *Caringbridge.org* to write my journal entries. I would update my site after each treatment or important event that took place. My formula was to make a theme out of it and make it more than just a medical update. I would often tell stories of who I met that day at the hospital, who was with me, and as you've seen so far, my "journal entries" are the backbone to this book. The sixty-five-plus trips I have made to the hospital, for various reasons, I was often accompanied by a friend or family member, my support group. As time went on, and people read my journal entries, their questions of how to help became questions like, "Can I drive you to treatment?" "Can I bring you lunch?" "Can I sit with you and keep you company?" "Can I pick you up and take you home?" Other times, people would just start doing things like dropping off dinner at our house. Sending gift cards in the mail. Offering up a mass in our name at their church. I even had people sending me books to read for inspiration and beautiful paintings and poems framed and given to me. Some of the gifts I received were from girls on my daughter's soccer team and my young cousin. Both little girls just happened to be named, Olivia. Olivia Leake and Olivia Holman. I literally received prayers, support, gifts and cards from people aged nine to ninety.

Another avenue we took to was *Facebook*. My wife was on it, and when I got sick, she made me get my own account. I also started an *Instagram* page. The good thing about these two is you can merge them. More importantly than anything else, the use of social media has reunited me with many people that I hadn't heard from in decades. Like anything in life, it's not for everyone, but used for the right reasons, social media is a great tool. You will find times during treatment that you will be too tired, sick or not in the mood for talking on the phone or answering texts.

Telling your story on a daily or weekly basis also opens the door for people to find out more about you. When that happens, your support group will find ways to help without asking, and that makes everyone more comfortable. I want to let everyone know right now that my intent was never about wanting or needing anything, and it was never about making me more comfortable. I understood what it's like to be on the other side of the table. I watched helplessly as friends died from this disease. I watched grandparents die from it when I wanted to do more. In particular, my maternal grandfather, Edward Lohmar. He and I were fairly close as far as grandson/grandfather goes. My middle name is Edward. It's hard to explain, but we seemed to have this quiet bond. In the spring of 1994 he was diagnosed with lung cancer. He knew he had cancer long before that. It was so advanced that he succumbed to the disease on June 24, 1994, so it didn't take long. I remember the time frame because I was caddying in the United States Open at Oakmont Country Club the week before he died. I knew he was very sick and in hospice, so I really wanted to get back home before he passed. I got back home on the 20th and was right by his side when he took his last breath. I was told he asked about me and where I was, so being there meant the world to me. I was the last one to feed him a spoonful of water. The more I age, the more cancer has been involved in my life. It will continue to be that way for me now that I have it. Unfortunately, until there is a cure, in all likelihood I will continue to know people who get diagnosed. We all must be our own advocate and take care of ourselves. Get annual checkups. Make others aware of what they need to do. Get involved with charities and promote fundraising for research. I will continue to be involved, and for the rest of my life, stay calm and kick cancer's ass. Lastly, maybe the best way to answer the question of, "What can I do to help?" is simply this. If you are a close friend or family member, make an appearance to show your concern and love for the person you call a friend. Sometimes just showing up is the best thing you can offer. Believe me, it made a big impact on me when friends and family stopped by the hospital or house.

A to Z

ONE OF MY OBJECTIVES TO WRITING ABOUT MY STORY WAS to keep it fairly short. Not sure that plan worked? I hope you aren't bored right now as you read this. I didn't set out to make this a long read, because the fact is, fighting cancer or any disease is about paying attention to the process. As I write this, I have no idea how many pages of a book this will be, but I want to make sure what is on each page is meaningful. So using the twenty-six letters of the alphabet, I have provided one word to focus on for each letter. Each of these words can help you whether you are battling cancer, a caregiver, a support person, or just living your life in general. These are all words and ideas I found to be of concern or more heightened to me since I got sick. I noticed myself and/or others around me needing or using these in the right and wrong ways. I continue to try and use these in positive ways to enrich my life and those around me.

Attitude. I wrote about this as being a main factor in my recovery. A positive attitude makes the road to recovery a little more tolerable.

Believe. If you don't believe in something, then how can you set any goals? This not only goes for an illness, but in all aspects of your life. We all set goals for things like losing weight, setting work goals, being a better friend, parent, a project around the house etc. If you don't believe in the goals you set, write them down, and look at them every day, then odds are you will fall short of the finish line.

Courage. Strength in the face of pain or grief. That is the definition of courage, but in our daily life, it's the courage to get from one moment in your life to the next.

Determination. What is your purpose in life? Find the strength to get there and let nothing stand in your way.

Empower. See A-D. Without control of your life, you can't set goals, reach goals, or make an impact on the people around you. I found this line by Steve Jobs that hit home with me: "Here's to the crazy ones, the misfits, the rebels, the troublemakers, the round pegs in the square holes, because the people who are crazy enough to think they can change the world, are the ones who do."

Faith/Family/Friends. I cheated here with three words because in life, you need all three. When you take all the minutia and clutter out of your life, the only things that matter are faith, family and friends.

Gratitude. Appreciate what you have and give what you can in return. We all tend to want more in our life. You want more? Give tenfold in return to what you get. Being grateful is much better than being greedy.

Hope. Probably the most famous line I can think of using the word "hope" comes from Stephen King: "Hope is a good thing, maybe the best of things, and no good thing ever dies." Hope is the buffer we use against impact of negative or stressful things we experience in life.

Inspire. Many friends and family have told me I've been an inspiration to them as I've battled my sickness. I'm thankful that is how they see me. How do you find inspiration in your life and what can you do to inspire others? My hope is to inspire people with this book to make their lives and those around them better.

Judicious. Not to be confused with being judgmental. Life can be a little easier on yourself and others when being prudent or using common sense. I liken this to having self-awareness. In other words, use the FIVE W's when speaking. Who are you speaking to? What are you saying to them? When are you saying it? Why are you saying it? Where are you when saying it?

Knowledge. Know things. This is a term some friends and I use. One of my nicknames is, "The Knower." I USED TO have a great memory of many things, but not so much anymore. However, I still try to learn and know as much as I can each and every day.

Love. Many times at a Catholic wedding, there is a verse from the book of *Corinthians* that is read. It is titled, "The Way of Love." In it is used the words, faith, hope and love, and I already have mentioned the previous two here. I will provide the condensed version. "Love is patient and kind; love does not envy or boast; it is not arrogant or rude. It does not insist on its own way; it is not irritable or resentful; it does not rejoice wrong-doing, but rejoices with the truth. Love bears all things, believes all things, hopes all things and endures all things. Love never ends. So now faith, hope and love abide, these three; but the greatest of these is Love." How much better would the world be if we all practiced this on a daily basis?

Meditate. There comes a time in your life when you will need to hit the "pause" button, especially when you are in the middle of treatments that may be zapping your mind and/or body of energy. When I say meditate, I'm not talking about going into a deep trance or chanting, but rather to just sit down alone in a room and just focus on one thing for about ten minutes. Or, don't focus on anything and just let your mind wander.

Never. Quite simply this word needs to be deleted from your vocabulary no matter where you are in life or what you are doing. We can't predict who or where we will be in the future, so to use the word "never" is coun-terproductive.

Open. Open yourself up to others. Open your heart to accept love and give love. Open your mind to new ways of thinking. Open your arms to hug someone. Open your wallet and open up time on your schedule to charitable giving. Open your eyes to see the good in people instead of the bad. Open up to the concept that you are mortal and your time on Earth

Passion. I was going to use the word "Positive" here, but I've stressed the importance of that word enough. Everyone has a passion for something. Find that passion that moves you. That excites you. It could be a sport, reading, traveling, watching movies, volunteering, cooking, philanthropy etc. Whatever it is, it must be true to yourself. You can't fake passion.

Quality. More than ever when battling a life threatening disease, the fear of the unknown is more pronounced. Unfortunately, it takes instances like this to realize you should be spending more quality time with the ones you love. Don't wait for that. Don't find excuses to delay that. I have relished the quality time I have spent with my friends and family who were there for me, even though some of them were forgotten during a period of my life.

Relax. Not everything is important even if you think it is. Don't sweat the small stuff. Your son or daughter staying out thirty minutes past curfew is not a reason to lose your shit. Sitting in a waiting room thirty minutes past your appointment time is not the end of the world. Trust me, when this happened, it only delayed my treatments even longer because my blood pressure was too high for chemotherapy. Then I had to RELAX to get it back down. 140/90 was my limit. Trust me, there were a few times I missed that mark.

Share. Whatever you know or have that can help others, share that with them. Offer but don't push. Share your time. Share your knowledge. Share your experience.

Trust. As a cancer patient, I was heading into the biggest question mark of my life. I found a quote written by Corrie Ten Boom that I remembered very early in my diagnosis. "Never be afraid to trust an unknown future to a known God." Corrie Ten Boom and her family helped many Jews escape the Nazis from the Holocaust by hiding them in their home.

Understanding. Understand your condition. Understand that sometimes things won't go as planned. Understand that each person battling cancer is different. Understand that others around you may not always understand your situation. Understand that this is a learning process for everyone in your life.

Value. Value what you have.

Why? Use this word with your doctor to question his or her direction of treatment plans. Never ask why me?

X-Factor. Keep a calendar during your treatments and mark an "X" on each day you met a goal. Keep a journal of your achievements.

You. You are loved. You are strong. You are the most important person to worry about in your fight against cancer.

Zest. Have a zest for life that comes through every day. Bring the enthusiasm but also enjoy it. All work and no play makes for a boring day.

Don't Ever

IF YOU ARE A CANCER PATIENT, DO AS I SAY, NOT AS I DO.
Although I'm not fat, drunk and stupid, I did play the part of stupid during a
hot summer day in July 2018. Oncologists and nurses will preach to you that
staying hydrated is very important during chemotherapy. Also, prolonged
periods of being out in the sun with your skin exposed is not wise either. That
advice went through one ear and out the other like my skull was nothing more
than a vast wasteland. My eighth grade teacher would argue that IS the case.
Anyway, I decided that mowing the lawn during a run of chemotherapy treatments was a good idea. So off I went with my little push mower, NOT self-
propelled, and began cutting away at my half-acre lot. Just picture some
scrawny nit wit in a baseball cap sweating his ass off and stopping every five
minutes. That was me. For over an hour, in ninety-degree heat, my dumbass
was out cutting grass. I think back and wonder, where the hell was my family?
On a vacation I didn't know about? That's a rhetorical question, because I'm
almost positive Colleen may have used the words: nuts, insane, dumb, stub-
born, and crazy ass when describing what I was about to do.

Needless to say, you can imagine what happened next. I completed the
job, because of course that was important, but then an onset of heat stroke and
dehydration set in. A trip to the hospital for about four hours of fluids got me
back in shape. I have since learned my lesson, because my neighbors, Kevin,
Becky and Bryan gifted me a pre-owned riding mower that they fixed up. Now
I tool around like Forrest Gump in my yard, but I don't use it to pick up the
mail or mow football fields.

Social media groups and blogs are nice to have. It allows you to have discussions with others in similar situations as you. However, don't ever base your health choices on what another cancer patient relays. As I've stated before, every patient reacts differently to drugs. Also, recommendations on what to take for side effects could have adverse reactions on your body. Always have a discussion with your oncologist before you put anything in your body. You should make sure to stay as positive as you can when having discussions on social media. I found myself straying away from them because some of the comments were all doom and gloom. I understand everyone has a different fight and stage of fight they are in, so please take that in consideration when making comments about yourself. These are supposed to be discussions about helping others, not discussions that lead others down the path of guilt, self-pity, and giving up.

One last thing I want to discuss in this chapter is happiness. Don't ever give up on the search for happiness. You won't find happiness in a checkbook or bank account, a car, a liquor bottle, a television show, a cell phone, a plate of food, or on a beach. Yes, those things will give you satisfaction, but they are all temporary. Bank accounts can eventually go to zero. Cars break down. A bottle eventually is left empty. Television shows have an end. Cell phones go out of style. Food can spoil. A beach erodes. Happiness is accepting what you have, knowing your limitations, and enjoying life with those you love. Those who love you will never leave you. There is no set price or value on happiness. Happiness is a state of mind. Happiness is waking up and seeing my wife lying next to me in bed. Happiness is a smile on my child's face. Happiness is knowing I have family and friends whom I love and who love me in return, unconditionally. Happiness is knowing that when you do leave this Earth, and you believe in God, then true happiness is waiting for you in Heaven. I know that's why my attitude and feelings toward cancer aren't conveyed in a negative light, because it's not ultimately in my power if this will be the deciding factor of my mortality. Was it a joyous or happy occasion when I got cancer? Hell no. Am I happy that some three years later I'm still here living life to the fullest? You bet I am! If you ever feel like you've lost your way or my words aren't making sense to you, then just go watch the movie *It's a Wonderful Life*.

Today is February 2, 2021. I'm currently on chemo treatment #47. I'm three years into my battle with cancer, and since I was given an 11 percent chance to live five years, things are looking good.

I now am thinking treatment may be what I deal with on a bi-weekly basis for the rest of my life. I try not to think like that, but human nature takes over and I need to fight it off. The emotional rollercoaster continues, and now more than ever, my family and friends are what we need most of all. We will lean on them when needed, but we also must focus on us as a family to stay bonded and lean on each of us to be stronger for each other.

Epilogue

MY HOPE IS TO BE BACK IN A FEW YEARS WITH A FOLLOW up book to tell you I'm a cancer survivor and how my support group and I have kicked this crap to the curb. I hope my story has provided you with some kind of enjoyment, enlightenment, and information, not only about cancer but also about life. Unfortunately, it took a devastating disease to open my eyes on how I was living my life. I still have a lot to learn, but I do know things are much more satisfying to me, and I no longer struggle with things out of my control. Make a difference and pay it forward as much as you can. I wrote this poem titled, "Legacy", as I was sitting in the hospital taking in my chemotherapy. Since none of us know our expiration date on this planet, it got me thinking, how will I be remembered?

When I look inside myself, what do I see? Hopefully, there's more there than just me.

Selfishness is holding onto things for your pleasure, but when you share them with others, there is no greater treasure.

Life can be lonely when you don't allow others in. So it's best to open your heart and let the fun begin.

God's gift of Love has no end. It's stronger than steel and will never bend. Once you accept His Love and pay it forward, your life will be instantly blessed and you will never be bored.

Your actions and words will be how you're remembered when your time has come. So do you want to be known as one who gave all or just gave some?

Stay safe and healthy. Listen to your body. Get your annual check-ups and get a colonoscopy as soon as you are eligible. If colon cancer is in your family history, you may be able to get one before age fifty. If you are experiencing any difficulties in life, whether it's physical or mental, seek help immediately. Reach out to a doctor, spouse, friend, anyone you feel comfortable talking with about your situation. Living in fear is not living at all. My hope is you will find what it is that makes you happy and healthy. My quest in Finding My Way will continue.

Stay safe and healthy,
Nick

Dedication

THIS BOOK DOESN'T HAPPEN WITHOUT THANKING SO MANY people. It all begins with my wife, Colleen. You are my best friend. My care-giver. The rock of the family. The love of my life who inspires me to be a better person. I love you so much that words just can't do it justice. I love you infinity times infinity. I never want you behind me or in front of me, because I need you right next to me.

I'm 99 percent confident that without Colleen, my story has a totally different outcome. I alluded to this earlier. In November of 1994, my life was stagnant. I was twenty-seven years old and heading nowhere. My career and life needed a complete overhaul. That Thanksgiving, I saw Colleen at a party. I didn't say, "Met her at a party" because I had known Colleen since 1975. You see, we went to elementary school together and grew up in the same Catholic parish of St. Clement in Des Peres, Missouri. We already knew each other from elementary school through high school. No, we never dated, but there was always a friendship in place. We struck up a conversation catching up on what each of us had been doing since high school. She had recently moved back to St. Louis after spending her college years in Springfield, Missouri, then working there and most recently, Memphis. Before the party ended, I asked her for her phone number. We went on our first date a month later on New Year's Eve.

Now twenty-one years later, we have four wonderful children. Drew, Eve, Grant and Tess. Where would my life be right now at fifty-three years old without them? God only knows. Without them, I'm not sure I could have battled cancer like I did. I found myself thinking about them and why I needed

5th grade. Me giving a thumbs up
with my future wife over my right shoulder.

My kids Christmas 2019. L to R: Grant, Eve, Tess and Drew.

to "win." My goals were simple. I didn't want to die because there was still so much I wanted to see my children accomplish. High school graduations, college graduations, their career choices, weddings and walking my two girls down the aisle, and Lord willing, grandchildren. Besides, Colleen and I still had a life that we wanted to complete.

I firmly believe that the mind is a powerful thing. The will to compete, win and live can take you down a path of success. My family provided that, and they were especially inspirational these last three years. And if you are battling cancer, or battling any other crisis in your life, lean on your family and friends. Get the support you need and don't be too proud to do just that. That is how I survived and continue to survive.

I thank my parents, Jerry and Ann, who have been there for me my entire life. Their sacrifices and love have given me so much. I want to also thank my in-laws, Gary and Mary Ellen, not only for their support the last twenty-five years, but for raising such a strong and beautiful woman.

I want to thank all my lifelong friends who I grew up with that pushed me into writing this, which include Shellie Smith Fahy, who was the final voice in my ear to get this done. Molly O'Neal Schad, Peggy Fitzgibbon, and Shellie Daly. All those who helped provide the funds to get this book published, including the entire St. Clement Class of 1982 and St. Louis University High Class of 1986. Thanks to the men who stood by me at my wedding. Michael Christian, Rob Maloney, John McMahon and my brother, Kelly. A special dedication to a childhood friend, Andy Bader. Andy was my first driving instructor who taught me how to drive a manual, or stick shift, as it's usually called. Fun times tooling around in my 1973 VW Beetle. Sadly, and suddenly, Andy passed away just a couple months before our first child was born. He is remembered every day by Colleen and I through our son, Andrew.

I thank my sisters, Julie, Regan, Amy and Holly. All my aunts, uncles, brothers in law, sisters in law, cousins, friends, friends of the family, parents of my friends, co-workers, and the doctors and nurses who saved my life. I thank our Twin Chimneys neighborhood "Sac" family. Every single person I know made an impact with their prayers, mass dedications, gifts, meals for my family, financial assistance and overall love you showed us. I know I can't list everyone here, but you all know who you are, and trust me when I say, you will never be forgotten. This book is dedicated to each and every person I know, because the path I've taken to get here was a path we all walked together at one time or another. Sometimes many, many times.

Thank you to those who have taken their time to read this book. No matter where you are in life, I hope this story brings some kind of enjoyment, education, information and/or assistance to your life. I hope it moves you in some degree emotionally.

My aunt Jani sent me a special letter one day written as always in beautiful calligraphy. In that letter was a saying from an unknown writer. Years ago it likely wouldn't have meant much to me, nor would I have really understood the meaning of it, but it all makes sense now.

"Our Family is a Circle of Love and Strength, with every birth and every union, the circle grows. Every joy shared adds more Love. Every crisis faced together makes the Circle stronger."

Team Porter...OUT

Our wedding day, November 13, 1999. Everyone in this photo was in the St. Clement 8th grade class from 1982. Friend then and still friends today.

CPSIA information can be obtained
at www.ICGtesting.com
Printed in the USA
LVHW081354041021
699482LV00002B/14